OLD LIVES: IN THE CHILCOTIN BACKCOUNTRY

JOHN SCHREIBER

Eagle Lake Henry Sill, Tex Hanson and Allietta Sill. Photo courtesy of Sage Birchwater.

OLD LIVES

IN THE CHILCOTIN BACKCOUNTRY

John Schreiber

CAITLIN PRESS
Halfmoon Bay, British Columbia

01 02 03 04 05 06 16 15 14 13 12 11

Caitlin Press Inc.
8100 Alderwood Road,
Halfmoon Bay, BC V0N 1Y1
www.caitlin-press.com

Editing by Audrey McClellan.
Text design by Kathleen Fraser.
Cover design by Vici Johnstone.
Printed in Canada

Caitlin Press Inc. acknowledges financial support from the Government of Canada through the Canada Book Fund and the Canada Council for the Arts, and from the Province of British Columbia through the British Columbia Arts Council and the Book Publisher's Tax Credit.

Canada Council   Conseil des Arts
for the Arts   du Canada

BRITISH COLUMBIA
ARTS COUNCIL
An agency of the Province of British Columbia

Library and Archives Canada Cataloguing in Publication
Schreiber, John, 1941–
        Old lives : in the Chilcotin backcountry / John Schreiber.

Includes bibliographical references.
ISBN 978-1-894759-55-7

        1. Country life—British Columbia—Chilcotin River Region. 2. Chilcotin River Region (B.C.). I. Title.

FC3845.C445S33 2011   971.1'75   C2011-900487-9

For Sage Birchwater, whose ready information, knowledge, generosity, inspiration and friendship were central to the creation of Old Lives;

for all those backcountry folks who persevered and survived;

and, as always, for Marne.

"Some story will come along and find these crows, and use them."

—Cree elder John Rains to William Muakos and Howard Norman after pondering the sight of ten dead and mangled crows on the snow in the bush near Gods Lake, northern Manitoba.

To the Cree, stories are animate beings. One could tell a biography of a single Cree story (which would be a story in itself) just as one could tell the natural history of an animal. In this respect, one could ask, What do stories do when they are not being told? Do they live in villages? Some Cree say they do. Do they tell each other to each other? Some Cree say this is true as well. Certainly stories live out in the world, looking for episodes to add to themselves. Therefore, we can understand John Rains's belief that eventually a story would find the torn crows. Later, that story would find a Cree person, inhabit that person awhile, and be told back out into the world again. A symbiotic relationship exists: If people nourish a story properly, it tells them useful things about life.

"Crow Ducks and Other Wandering Talk"
Howard Norman
in *The Language of the Birds*
David M. Guss, ed.

Photo courtesy of Damon West Photography.

CONTENTS

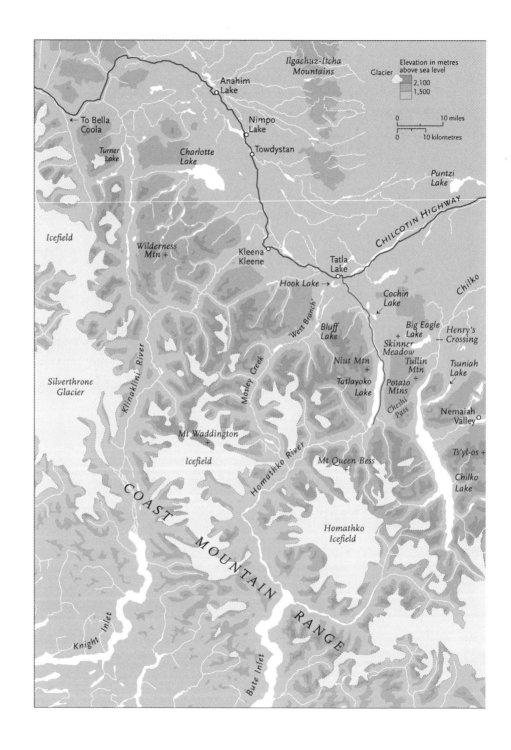

Glacier

Elevation in metres
above sea level
2,100
1,500

0   10 miles
0   10 kilometres

*Ilgachuz-Itcha
Mountains*

Anahim
Lake

→ To Bella
Coola

Nimpo
Lake

Towdystan

*Puntzi
Lake*

*Turner
Lake*

*Charlotte
Lake*

CHILCOTIN HIGHWAY

Icefield

*Wilderness
Mtn* +

Kleena
Kleene

Tatla
Lake

Chilko

Hook Lake →

*Cochin
Lake*

*Bluff
Lake*

'West Branch'

*Big Eagle
Lake*
+

*Henry's
— Crossing*

*Skinner
Meadow*

Niut Mtn
+

*Tullin
Mtn*
+

*Tsuniah
Lake*

*Silverthrone
Glacier*

Klinaklini River

Mosley Creek

*Tatlayoko
Lake*

*Potato
Mtns*

*Chezhi
Pass*

*Nemaiah
Valley* ○

Mt Waddington
+

Homathko River

Mt Queen Bess
+

Ts'yl-os +

Icefield

*Chilko
Lake*

*Homathko
Icefield*

C O A S T

M O U N T A I N

Knight Inlet

R A N G E

Bute Inlet

Map by
Eric Leinberger.
Courtesy of
New Star Books.

INTRODUCTION: OLD LIVES

Listen.
This living flowing land
is all there is, forever
We are *it*
It sings through us—

"By Frazier Creek Falls"
—Gary Snyder

THROUGHOUT MOST OF 1965, I worked at Mahatta River, a logging camp situated inside the mouth of Quatsino Sound on the far northwest coast of Vancouver Island. I ran a dozer boat on the booming and barge-loading grounds or laboured out on the rigging as a hooktender, the boss of a log-yarding crew. We were on one of the last of the high-lead, wooden spar tree-and-winch set-ups, a technology developed and refined in the railroad-logging days of the 1920s, '30s and '40s. Those so-called glory days took place in the wide, warm, Douglas fir valleys down Island, but up at Mahatta, in the grey and wet, we were logging hemlock, cedar and Sitka spruce.

Sometimes out there, as turns of logs were yarded to the landing and rainstorms blew by, I would gaze across at the contours of the land we were working on and the tree-covered hills beyond. Wispy cloud fragments and tendrils, like tiny bomb-bursts, would scud in steadily off the open saltchuck to the west. And usually there were ravens doing loop-de-loops in the updrafts, eyeing our lunch boxes and calling each other names.

As the weeks and months passed, I came to feel those places we were in as deep places, redolent of something timeless, something powerful. I could sense that this land we were stripping the timber off was not inanimate but alive, sentient, vital, and I was becoming touched by it, indelibly. That knowing was in my bones. Old memories of the mouth of the Cluxewe River on the east side of the Island, an open estuary near Port McNeill, where I grew up, would come frequently to mind. The Cluxewe was a favourite spot, a Shangri-la for us when we were young, and we went there often to fish, dig clams, hunt ducks, or simply enjoy the openness and history of the place. I remembered standing on the spit and staring up the coastline to the northwest at the headlands fading off into mist, wondering how the original inhabitants might have seen them and thinking that our apparently different ways of seeing must overlap in some manner. It was here in the damp that my watchful spirit got lit on fire.

In later years, as I reflected back on those early knowing moments, I realized that it was a myth awareness I'd been dipping into, and that this "myth time" I'd been reading about in anthropology texts at university did not occur way back then in some hazy time before time, but happens right here, right now, and always will.

Of course, the first aboriginal peoples came here in the wake of the glaciers over ten thousand years ago, or even earlier perhaps, in "time immemorial" as some would say. There were the familiar signs, so common up and down the coast, of their long presence at Cluxewe mouth: deep, black-earth, white-clamshell middens at the base of the spit; an old summer village site, Lex.si'we ("clover root/bar on river mouth") by name; and ancient, half-rotted hulks of stumps off in the woods. If a land could be said to belong to humans at all, then this northwest land was theirs until recently, when we settlers came along in great numbers from over the seas to share it with them, uninvited and largely oblivious of the severity of our impact on those original inhabitants.

Now I've come to see the reverse to be the truth: that it is we, all of us, aboriginal and non-aboriginal, whether we choose to admit and act on it or not, who are subsidiary to this land where we live, and not the other way around. We are composed of and informed by this great Earth we stand and walk on, and when we die, one way or another we die back into it. To the extent that we humans cease to see ourselves as the epicentre of existence, we may become intelligent. I hope we are now embarked on the task of learning to co-exist equitably and sensitively in this place where we are.

It seems to me that the real cultural gulf out here in the West is not so much a racial as a rural/urban split, the separation between those with earth under their feet and those with concrete; those who know which watershed they are in and where the weather comes from, and those for whom, generally, such knowledge seems unimportant. These differences as to where we live are to some degree also about, and exacerbated by, the issue of class—"them that has [power and wealth] and them that don't"—although political and economic limitations are obviously not confined to country people.

The gap between the rural and the urban, these two basic ways of being and seeing in this province and across the West, is widening, the gulf between deepening. The two cultures are basically different, and folks in the second, the urban culture, even many of those in it who claim to be environmentally sensitive, have virtually no conception of the rural minority at all. Country people mostly know who city people are; it is in their self-interest, as a minority, to do so. Somewhere in their awareness of themselves, though, the majority of rural folks, whether from up the coast or the Interior, know they are land-based; the shape and nature of land and its effects are self-evident all around them. Most urbanites take little time in their typically busy and distracted lives to notice much of their surroundings, to know which way the waters flow and the winds blow. A friend, Joy Schilling from Darfield, up the North Thompson River north of Barriere, said to me a while back: "Sometimes I have the feeling that the people down there [in the cities of southwestern BC] do not know *where* they are."

I've lived my adult life in both cultures, but my upbringing was near totally and profoundly rural. When I was a young boy at Darfield, I was immersed in, and became attached to, the Interior world of quaking poplar leaves, dry air, cold winters, coyotes and wilderness for a few years after the war, when my father was attempting to guide-outfit for a living. Then, in 1951, as the bills accumulated, he went back logging, and we moved, my mother loyally accepting yet another change, to Port McNeill. As teenagers and young adults, my brothers and I worked in various logging camps around the north end of Vancouver Island and up in Haida Gwaii—the Queen Charlottes as they were referred to then.

Like our father before us, we grew up to understand and appreciate the place and culture we were in, the relatively self-sufficient, land- or sea-based world of loggers, fishermen and, in earlier days, homesteaders (known to coast folks then as "stump ranchers"), all trying to make a living in a powerful and daunting environment. The weather, climate and seasons, and the lay and contours of the land were working, living realities to us, affecting strongly and minutely all our activities, day to day, hour to hour.

With the disappearance of the old made-at-home, labour-intensive, wooden spar tree technology, and the advent of steel spars, track loaders, dozer boats and lightweight no-stop power saws in the early to mid-sixties, the locus of logging intelligence shifted from the logging camps to Vancouver, Seattle and New York, and the key issues in the business of forestry became increasingly abstract. With the coming of TV and roads linking us to the lower Island (which we knew as "down Island'), and with the disappearance of bunkhouses and cookhouses, the culture changed; it shrank quickly and all but disappeared, even before we logged off most of the timber.

What we had up to that time on the northwest coast was a unique but short-lived (maybe four generations) post-contact, land-based culture. Most of those up-coast folks, whether aboriginal or recent immigrants, were central to their own existence and knew, and were proud of, who they were and what they could do. Work was hard, survival was often difficult, perseverance, toughness and a wide range of skills were necessary, but there was art in it, in much of the work and in survival both. Although few of us would have given up the accessibility, comfort and entertainment of the new reality, the price was paid, and the old way of life is gone like wood smoke up the chimney, nothing left but a few sparks in the night sky. Now most of us in this fast, surprisingly isolated city-world never knew we had such a way of life of value to lose, let alone miss and mourn. As the fisherman father of a friend of mine said, "Yeah, we've seen the best of her."

So in the late sixties and early seventies, when I began coming into the Cariboo–Chilcotin country, I soon realized that, in some ways, I already had a clear sense of the lay of the cultural terrain up there. Instead of spar trees, steep sidehills, caulk boots and driving rain to deal with, up in the central Interior there are cows, horses, long cold snowy winters and short growing seasons. Both cultures knew mosquitoes, logging trucks, and the value of clean-flowing creek water; both experienced isolation. And both cultures lived the same kind of self-sufficient, autonomous way of life, directly connected to the ground we walked, rode or drove around on. The topography at hand was either in our favour or not, and if it was not, we adapted, but it was never a factor to ignore. The same was true for weather. If something broke, we got out or down or off and fixed it, at least enough to keep going. Up the coast, we called that "haywiring." "She's a gunny sack show" meant it was a tenuous fix but probably enough to get us through.

Up in the Cariboo–Chilcotin there are folks—the extended Schuk family; the McGhees in the old days; the Butlers over at West Branch; the Lulua sisters and brother Casimil at Tullin Ranch by Chilko Lake; the Squinas family up at Anahim; Veera Bonner's people around Big Creek; the Kosters, Grinders, Pigeons and Twans over on the Cariboo side; the Menhinicks down in Gold Bridge; all these and many more—who are, or were, people who knew something. They knew how to survive, think, be strong and creative, enjoy their solitude and, mainly, get along. I know too well that life in the far corners of the backcountry, coast or Interior, can get small, really small, and tight at times. Sometimes it stays that way, but at the very least these folks knew where they lived and how they fit in. The best, usually the older ones, even knew who they were. In Cormac McCarthy's *No Country for Old Men*, a character, the main narrator in the story, states: "My daddy always told me … there was nothin to set a man's mind at ease like wakin up in the morning and not havin to decide who you were."

Predictably, in these fast times, that old slow way of life up there is shifting; it was bound to. But in this era of radical forgetting, where so many are mesmerized by small shiny digital objects, instant gratification and excess, and where the differences between wisdom, knowledge and information are blurred, all those (mostly) competent and practical old-time rural people need to be remembered and acknowledged. It is the elders, in particular, reared in such different and often trying times, who deserve our recognition and respect for surviving and making a reasonable living for themselves and their families. For whatever reason—intelligence and attitude or lack of heavy technology—their impact on this land has been light. Nowadays, they and most of their progeny are scattered but are carrying on across the land, probably telling a few tales and having a laugh or two doing it. To the extent that they were together and endured well, these folks are heroes. This is us I am talking about. This is the land and these are the people that shaped this west-of-the-Rockies culture of ours out here.

And this may be the beginnings of myth talk I'm touching on, these stories of where we live and who we are. Mythology is about wisdom. And for all their usefulness, our super technologies are not. We newcomers lack and sorely need an informing mythology that is of and from this place. No one can set out to create a myth, but we can facilitate the process by staying open to possibilities and by persuading short-sighted, self-focused ego to step out of the way. In doing so we might come to experience the wild, beautiful liveliness that is in all things and that is the lifeblood of free-run myth. Joseph Campbell said: "Myth opens the world to the dimension of mystery, to the realization of mystery that underlies all forms." Mystery, like mythology, can only ever be wild.

For myself, even a glancing sense of the experience and power of mythologizing helps to get me through. I could not touch the souls of these Chilcotin stories and of the old lives depicted in them without it.

WHERE WE COME FROM

It all boils down to who dropped you, and where.

—Andy Russell

THERE ARE QUIET, little places around this province where lives go on, on their own, sometimes in old-time ways. Nobody much knows about these locations, except for the people who live there, or relatives and friends, maybe, from more urban settings or other rural parts. There are small pockets of people scattered here and there, at the ends of roads or on alternate routes, often gravelled, that are less travelled by far than the fast throughways with the loud transport trucks heading east, the vans and SUVs with their automatic transmissions, air conditioning and hunched, white-knuckled drivers, eyes intent on the yellow line.

It was on a side road in such a place on a sunny spring morning, some years back, that my partner, Marne, took some photographs of three First Nations men on horses; one of a small, but carefully built, old dormered house, burnt nearly black by the sun, and sporting doors and window frames painted turquoise; and another of a low church close by, even smaller and darker than the house. Marne, in her usual charming way, promised the main horseman, a big, quietly authoritative, seemingly ageless man, that she would get the developed photos back to them.

The old church at Thirty Mile. Photo courtesy of Marne St. Claire.

The other two riders, both young lean men, watched, listening, the one straight-faced in ball hat, reflector glasses and wide moustache; the other just there.

The next year I returned, without Marne this time, but with five clear colour prints, four by sixes, to find those men and give the pictures to them. After a long, slow, sunny drive, spotting birds, places, signs of old lives and indicators of spring, I found the small remembered gathering of old houses, barns and fences on a sloping sidehill. There was the tiny church—derelict, I think—with that burnt-brown, antiquated look, sinking down into itself, farther up the hill behind. I looked for a particular house where, on that earlier trip, heavy metal rock music had reverberated and a young man had stood on the front porch yelling down to us and to the world at large across the cool sunlit hillside, announcing his own angry, diminished presence, I suppose. I walked up to the gate, lifted the chain off the horseshoe nail on the post and approached the house.

A small, grey-haired woman came out to meet me. She asked, a bit suspiciously, "Are you lost?"

I said I wasn't but that my wife, Marne, had taken pictures of three guys on horses near here and had promised to send copies to them. Now I needed help identifying them.

"Come in," she said.

I followed and entered her house. The place was neat. There were several people seated, eating preserved fruit and chocolate cake. A baby had just slid down between the bars of a fine, old, ornate steel bedstead used as a couch, planted firmly in the middle of the room. He looked a little bewildered but made no fuss. My host, Sarah Ann, pointed to another couch covered with a bright, hand-knitted afghan. "Have a seat."

She extricated the baby, took the proffered photographs, examined them quickly and closely (I think she was a little short-sighted), then passed them around. I retold the story of my quest to the others: Francis, a middle-aged man in glasses with faint tattoos up and down his arms and hands; fine-featured Georgina, mother of the baby, at the table by the window; and young Jordan, about six, clear-faced, obviously the older brother of the infant. Francis thought they were nice pictures, "real clear," he said. I told him Marne had liked these photos also.

Sarah Ann identified the men in the pictures as Roger Hance and his brother David. The third guy, Darryl, was a friend of theirs. Then she asked me if I would like some fruit. She said she had preserved it herself.

I did not want to bother them at their get-together and, as politely as I could, declined her offer. Sarah Ann, who had been cautious at first, was now warm-eyed. The others nodded and smiled except for the sixth member of the group, who was silent and sitting close by me at the table, intent on finishing his dessert, his broad back turned, in what seemed like an endless expanse of bright white T-shirt. He had a strong neck, short bristly hair and Indian ears, lobes out.

From the far end of the table, Georgina said that the church in the picture was the one up the road at Thirty Mile. "Same as the house."

The big man turned, looked at the pictures with care, then proceeded to talk affably, telling me that he'd taken a bunch of pictures himself and had some of them made into a calendar. That was it, in fact, hanging on the wall, right behind the bedstead. He invited me to take it down and have a good look. There were pictures of horses and dead deer and bighorn sheep heads, and his and Georgina's kids, Jordan and little Tim Junior, who, of course, were right here in the room. I asked where the sheep were from, and he replied that they were from around Lytton. Marne and I had seen good numbers of bighorn sheep near the mouth of Botanie Creek, north of Lytton, on several occasions. They would be introduced Rocky Mountain bighorns, relatively new to that lower Thompson River country, and darker and more stocky than Californias, in my observation. The mature rams have a tighter, thicker curl to their horns. Marne was able to take good pictures of several ewes at the side of the road. Some young rams had been grazing on a treed bench below us. When they opted to depart the place, they took off at instant full speed, powering their way

Bighorn ewes above Botanie Creek near Lytton. Photo courtesy of Marne St. Claire.

up the hillside with those big, muscled, rear haunches of theirs, quickly out of sight.

Georgina told me that she tried to arrange the pictures in the calendar according to the month and season. She seemed to be making an effort to explain things, to make sure I understood. I said I thought that the calendar was a nice way to preserve memories.

There was one picture of the baby in a huge black cowboy hat. I said to serious Jordan, who was looking over my arm, that I thought the baby's hat was way too big. He didn't crack a smile, nor did anyone else. There was another picture of two men, one holding a baby, on a pinto horse with saddlebags behind the saddle. It was not a big pinto horse.

"That pinto tried to buck us off," big Tim said. He then told me his name was Tim Voght and proceeded to carefully spell out his surname for me. I recognized that last name but couldn't place it.

I was not surprised that the small pinto had tried to dump its heavy load. Tim pointed to the man with the child and said he had jumped off right away. The baby he had been holding was Tim Junior.

There was another picture of Tim, wading across a small river, the autumn sun shining through the yellow cottonwood leaves behind him. He explained that he had been chasing a moose and that he got wet feet. "At least he got something," Georgina said with a big smile. I laughed, a bit overly loudly I felt.

"That name, Hance?" I asked. "There's an old pioneer family with that name in their back history up in the Chilcotin country. They settled near to what became Lee's Corner. Any connection?"

"Nope," Tim said quickly. Francis then took pains to point out to me that his last name was Adams and that there were lots of Adamses around Kamloops, but none of them was related to him, not one.

I thought to myself: I'll bet there's a connection. Hance is not a common name. How many Hances could there be in this province?

"Have some fruit," Sarah Ann said. She listed the cherries and strawberries and a few huckleberries in the dessert and stated that she had made the cake herself. She passed me an ornately iced section of chocolate cake in an aluminum foil pan.

"I can't resist," I said. "Did you grow the cherries yourself?"

She gestured out the window and said she had, "From that tree out there." The tree was not yet in full leaf.

"Did you grow the strawberries?" Again she pointed outside to a big fenced plot, freshly dug, damp, dark earth, ready for seeding, and replied that she had, "In that garden right there. Did you get enough?"

"Oh yeah," I said, "quite enough." I heard Francis laugh gently behind me. The dessert was really good and I had eaten quickly, carefully placing the cherry pips on my knee until I was finished.

Tim Voght announced that he had a ranch south of Merritt and about thirty horses. That's a lot of horses to feed.

"On the Coldwater River?" I asked.

He nodded.

"Voght?" I said, finally remembering the name. "Isn't there a Voght Lake around there somewhere?"

Tim corrected me, saying it was Voght Valley and that it was his great-great-grandfather who had homesteaded there. It is about twenty miles south of Merritt, and William Henry Voght had settled in the area about the time the railroad was being built through Spence's Bridge. Voght Valley was where the Widow Smith, the famous Spence's Bridge apple grower, first settled when she and her husband came in to this country at about that same time, accompanied by the young James Teit.

"Hey," I said to Tim, "you're a man of the country," and immediately felt my quick words sounded slightly foolish. Of course, he was a man of the country; the Voghts around Coldwater had been people of that country long before they were Voghts. Tim laughed, kind of proudly.

I told them I was headed up to the Chilcotin, to Fletcher Lake in fact, near Big Creek, south of Lee's Corner. Tim said he used to work on that big ranch on the way in. He'd worked there as a cowboy for three years a while back. He claimed to have combed every bit of that bush around Big Creek, looking for cows.

"Would that be Chilco Ranch?" I asked.

He nodded and said that when he worked there they called him Bulldog—whether after the rodeo routine or because of his stubborn qualities, I was not certain. He urged that if I went past the ranch to the gas station on nearby Stone Reserve, I should be sure to look up the couple who runs that place; they were good friends of his. "Tell 'em you were talking to Bulldog," he said.

I stated that I was probably going down to the Nemaiah Valley, way south past Stone Reserve. Tim remarked that he'd been down the mine road that branches farther south, just short of the Elkin Creek bridge at the entrance to Nemaiah. He'd seen the far end of Taseko Lake, and the airstrip at the outlet of Fishem Lake near there. I remembered the long, muddy, potholed road and the big snowy mountains to the west and south and east of the head of Taseko Lake. I'd crossed that rough gravel runway and spotted old kekuli, pithouse holes, on a little point between the runway and the edge of Fishem. I'd first been down there seventeen years earlier.

> *I remembered the long, muddy, potholed road and the big snowy mountains to the west and south and east of the head of Taseko Lake.*

"I am intrigued by history," Tim Voght said.

"Me too," I replied. "I'm the same. That's why I come up these back roads, to see the history."

Tim said he had one of those old wagon wheel-tighteners. They clamp around the outside of the wheel to squeeze the spokes in tight. Did I know what it was he was talking about? He liked to go through old garbage piles to see what was there. I presumed he was referring to prowling around old shacks and homesteads and mine sites, and agreed with him completely. There are few activities more interesting and there's always more to learn.

Tim told me about the time he'd tried to drive all the way home to Merritt on back roads, and he'd just about made it—until he had to cross the Trans-Canada Highway. As he spoke, I recalled Gordon Antoine, from Coldwater, a sociable man I'd worked for in the early seventies. Tim must surely have known him, probably very well.

"So, where does Roger Hance live?" I asked.

Georgina replied that the Hances were just down the road, about three miles back from where I'd come. They had a big name sign nailed to a fir tree on the uphill side that I couldn't miss. "You just drive up that side road until you get to his house," she said. "You'll probably hear that big laugh of his." I remembered the sign.

Sarah Ann suddenly asked where my wife was. She sounded worried and half rose to look out the window. She hoped Marne wasn't out there sitting and waiting in my car.

Trying to make a little joke, I replied that Marne was down in Victoria, working away at her teaching job, while I was up here seeing the country and having fun. I hesitated, then added, "She's just getting over breast cancer surgery."

Sarah Ann said that she'd read about this surgery. Was Marne okay? Was she going to get better? There was real hurt in her voice as she asked.

I replied that it looked like Marne was going to be all right. There was no history of cancer in the family, and she wasn't overweight—that is to say, she didn't carry much fat. The doctors had caught the tumour early and it was small, slow-growing and shaped like a dime. It wasn't one of those cancer tumours that spread explosively like little bombs. They cut out some of her lymph nodes and found them clear, but her arm was numb and would be that way for a while.

There was a pause.

"Cancer is spooky," I said. "It's kind of like having a ghost on your shoulder."

Nobody spoke. I announced that it was time for me to go, that I had to deliver those pictures before it got dark. "Thanks for the excellent dessert, and I'm glad to have met you."

"Tell them we sent you," Georgina said.

I backtracked, found the Hance sign, drove up the winding side road, parked on the hill by a rail gate, walked through, and found myself on a good-sized, sloping, cultivated bench facing east, with eight or nine horses of all colours grazing on a steep bunchgrass mound up behind. There were three houses, one above me and two below, right beside me. There was a fourth home farther down the slope, accessible from a different road. I walked to the closer of the two houses below me to knock on the door. A tractor was coming down the hill, raising dust at the top of the field. It was about suppertime. The sun was weak and low, the shadows long and the wind blowing chilly. Little dust swirls blew off the yard.

I knocked on the door again. A TV was blaring. There were kids inside. Nobody answered. A man in glasses and blue turtleneck shirt was watching me from the window of the next house below. I waited a little, then walked over. A saddled horse, a bay, was hitched by its halter rope to a fence rail. Its bridle was hanging off the pommel. There was the butt of a rifle, looking the length and butt-shape of a Winchester 30-30, sticking out of the saddle scabbard. The man came out to meet me. I explained quickly about Marne's promise and that I was looking for Roger or David Hance.

"Come in," he said.

I went in. The place was well kept. There were dozens of family photos pasted to one wall. A television about the size of a D-4 Cat was on in the corner; some game-show host was saying something smooth, accompanied by the usual automatic laughter. There was a sharp smell like smoked fish, not unpleasant.

I showed the pictures to the man. He resumed his seat in the window to look at them. Something was frying in the kitchen; fat was snapping and crackling. Another odour came to me, pungent and a bit too rich. Something about it took me back to my early childhood days in the Interior when, out of necessity and our closeness to the bush, our family ate a lot of deer and moose meat. I remembered loving to eat well-fried deer liver, eating too much and getting thoroughly sick and put off liver forever.

An older woman walked in, smiling, small, her grey hair up around her head. I retold my story briefly. The young man passed the pictures of the riders to her. The lady, still smiling, got out her glasses and studied the photos intently.

"Yeah, that's us," the man said. I said that I hadn't recognized him from the pictures. The man in the blue shirt was the long-faced Hance brother with the reflector glasses in the photo. He twinkled, a touch ruefully I thought. He had the same wide moustache.

The smiling lady proclaimed that those were her sons: this was David Hance here in the room, and that was Roger Hance coming down the hill. "They're the Hance boys," she said proudly.

I showed them the picture of the house with the turquoise door and

The house where Mrs. Hance lived as a child. Photo courtesy of Marne St. Claire.

window frames and the one of the little, low, sun-burnt church. Mrs. Hance told me she grew up in that painted house. That was her childhood home. "Well, you should have them then," I said.

Big Roger in a red ball hat and well-worn blue jean jacket, buttoned to the neck against the evening cool, walked in. His bulk indicated a padded vest underneath. He ignored us as he disappeared to put his stuff away, then returned to the room a little later. I told the story all over again

WHERE WE COME FROM

and showed him the pictures. He took them and looked at them quickly. He seemed tired and a bit bewildered, probably numb from sitting on his tractor all day, and was obviously ready to eat. He stuck his hand out and shook mine with that old-time, gentle contact, his hand barely touching mine. I had learned a long time ago not to knuckle-crunch. Roger's hand was a lot bigger and rougher than mine. He thanked me and gave me a fast look of gratitude, maybe of relief, something vulnerable in his black eyes. I told them that I wished them all a good evening and quickly left. I was glad I had returned the images to them.

On the way back up the road, I thought about that name, Hance, again. I had seen it on a street sign just off the highway down south, below Lytton. I thought of the old days, when aboriginal people sometimes took on the name of some significant settler, for any of several possible reasons. Oft times, an early settler or fur company employee had two families— the first, the Indian one, his "country marriage" as some called them; then, later, the second, non-Indian marriage—with offspring from both. It was not uncommon for the second family to have no knowledge at all of the existence of the first family, but the first would know all about the second. So, most likely, would the rest of whatever community there was around. There are stories, some amusing, some bitter, stemming inevitably from those "country" complications. And frequently, as the impact of the new settler culture became overwhelming, especially as the indigenous languages were discouraged, those first children of Indian mothers would take on the surname of the missing or never-present father, now moved on to supposedly more fertile pastures.

Often, over the generations, particularly if they continued to live in the same region, the two sets of descendants would come to recognize, know and accept one another; sometimes not. Family reunions have

33

taken place, over the decades, attended by aboriginal and settler descendants alike. There are apparently non-Indian folks, frequently old ranch families, with Indian faces, and there are First Nations people with first-settlers' surnames and first-settlers' faces in small towns and backcountry places all over this province and, I suppose, most other provinces and territories in this fair Dominion.

It is not just long-ago relationships, marriages and old blood that link aboriginal and settler descendants. Irrevocably, over time, as people lived their lives together on the same land and shared the same demands of weather, season, occupation, isolation, privation and basic survival, they would come to know, appreciate and depend on each other.

I think of Veera Bonner at Fletcher Lake, herself a descendant of the original Hance at Hanceville, just down the road from Lee's Corner. That man, Tom Hance, was her grandfather. At times, in her earlier winters at Fletcher Lake, Veera was there alone but for Juliana Setah, daughter of the wandering Chiwid, and Juliana's husband, Willie George, on the far side of the lake. I heard Veera exclaim, more than once, how reassuring and heart-warming it was, in that white and frozen world, to see that small, welcome light glowing in their cabin window on a dark evening. She knew if she needed help, or if her lamp didn't light up at dusk as it should, she could count on her neighbours for support. And she would gladly do the same. It did not matter who they were.

I passed a small car, coming my way. It was Georgina and Tim Voght, and the children, probably heading home. Georgina, who was driving, waved her hand rapidly, almost excitedly, as if to be sure to catch my attention. Tim, a large still shadow in the passenger seat, was wearing his black hat, about twenty gallon, minimum, I'd say—the same great hat that had sat on Tim Junior's little head in the calendar picture. It filled the car. I couldn't see the kids.

A few minutes later, I approached the house where Sarah Ann and Francis were. The shadows were long and the front window blank, but I knew they'd be there, sitting at either end of the kitchen table. I rolled down my window and gave a long, long-armed wave. Instantly, two hands returned the wave, very busy, from either side of the window. I could see the palms of their hands clearly.

I drove on up north. Marne always said, "Go do something for somebody else." I remembered Francis Adams gently smiling. It was a good evening to be living.

A year or two after that, about mid-May, I was travelling down that same slow back road, south this time. I was driving the same dark red 4x4 as on my previous visitation. It was a beautiful sunshine morning; the lilacs around the old homesteads and the places where old homestead houses used to be were in heavy, purple, redolent bloom. The air was clear and cool, inviting in the shadows and low places, and touched with the smell of spring. I came to the sloping hillside and the little gathering of buildings that included Sarah

It is not just long-ago relationships, marriages and old blood that link aboriginal and settler descendants.

Ann's house and pulled over, stopping by the pasture fence, briefly, to look across, remember and dream a little. The cherry tree was blooming. Her garden plot would have been ready for seeding.

As I sat watching, a hand, behind the glass at the far side of the big front window, pulled the curtain to one side and held it. The sun's angled morning light illuminated the hand and slim wrist, and the adjacent curtain material. After an extended minute, the hand was withdrawn into shadow. The curtain fell back into place.

A SHORT WALK IN THE POTATO MOUNTAINS

Within and around the earth,
within and around the hills,
within and around the mountain,
your authority returns to you.

Tewa prayer

SO HERE WE go again.

We are walking up the slopes at the south end of the Potato Mountains on the southwestern edge of the Chilcotin Plateau. This time it's mid-September and snow is falling. It's been coming down in fits and starts for a couple of days now. We are in timber still; there is snow on the ground around us, and more snow on low fir branches hanging heavily over the trail, that I knock off with my stick as we pass. Snowflakes drift about as if not sure where to land. Tree trunks are presences brooding, dark and silent; all else is white. My brother Chris is sauntering along in his usual easy way, some distance behind me, the deep woods absorbing what little sound he makes. Chris is not one to talk when he walks. In all the many years I have travelled in high places with him, I have seldom seen or heard him breathe hard (in contrast to myself), and I continue to be curious as to how he does it.

We have come to this Tatlayoko Lake country for views of sunlit peaks and perhaps some mountain photographs in autumn shades of red and golden, though the calendar tells us it is the season of summer still. Half a day after our arrival, the snow began falling, and by evening there was a foot of it on the hillsides above the road along the valley. The mountains across from Iris Moore's cabin, near the head of the lake, and south down the Homathko River, deep in the heart of the Coast Range, are blanketed in soft thick white except for a few exposed rock faces. My previous September trips to this area had been sunny, if not always warm, and wonderfully pleasant. But winter comes early in these mountains if it feels so inclined. And the day following, as we stand on the porch of the Tatla Lake store up on the main highway, noting the continuing snowfall and chatting, local rancher Joe Schuk tells me, with the knowing of a long lifetime in this country, "It'll snow just about any month of the year but August around here."

We have come to this Tatlayoko Lake country for views of sunlit peaks and perhaps some mountain photographs in autumn shades of red and golden.

Chris and I thought we might start up the stock trail to the main ridge of the Potatoes to see how far the snow would allow us to climb and if maybe the sky would lighten up enough for us to take a picture or two up there on high. These were the mountains where, in the old days not so long ago, aboriginal people gathered to dig "soont'ih" (Indian potatoes), otherwise called spring beauty, and to hunt deer, rodeo, socialize and have a good time. They would ride their horses or walk up access trails from the northeast and northwest, much like this steep southern track we are walking on now.

When Chris and I drove down the lake earlier in the morning, the valley was thick with low cloud. Cows were bunched up at the cattle guards, waiting for their rancher, Les Harris I believe, to open the gates and let them through so they could make their way back up-valley to the home pastures around his place. The multitude of tracks and poop-plops in the wet mud along the roadside told us they'd been here for a while.

Now, as we push our way up and across the hillside, more white-faced bovines appear out of the dark, lightless timber in front of us. They are silent and walking with purpose, all aimed in the same direction, down, out of the high country, pushed on by "the big white cowboy," cold and relentless, above them. They move in small family groups past us, led by smart old broody cows, who have been here before and know the routes. Some pause to stare, turning their heads to check us out. Their wide-assed calves are so fat, their butt ends jiggle when they run. Some calves are wild and spooky, and for most this is their first brush with two-leggeds walking—a challenging sight, especially a couple of contrary, oldish farts, mulishly headed off and up in the opposite direction.

Judging from the tracks angling across the snow at the start of the first steep, semi-exposed hillside farther along, some cattle overnighted in the open, getting what protection they could in the lee of clumps of whitebark pine and stubby, high-elevation lodgepoles. At daylight they lit out of there; their tracks are fresh. Deer tracks are pointed downhill also, looking tentative and delicate among the broad cow prints. The deer, mostly does and half-grown fawns, left the hillside at an earlier part of the dawn than the cattle, headed straight down, probably to the horse pastures around Bracewell's lodge in Cheshi Pass.

We discover quickly that we'll likely manage the entire trail, right to the ridge top, 2,000 to 3,000 feet above us, without undue effort. The snow on the trail under our feet is, except for a few shaded spots, a mere four or five inches deep; it is a foot or more everywhere else across the slope. Prior to the recent snowfall, the late August weather had been hot, and the open, south-facing, dark-earth trail would have been deep-down warm, causing a partial melt. Even with switchbacks the walking is steep, but the ground is hard, the air nippy and the conditions comfortable, not nearly so tiring as if it had been a hot day. There is thin cloud cover above us, and low fog in Cheshi Pass and down the creek past Bracewell's below us, as well as out over Tatlayoko Lake, but the sun is beginning to show fleeting, watery glimpses of itself. Patches of bald stone faces are opening up to the southeast on Huckleberry Mountain, a compact humpy mountain above Chilko Lake between us and Stikelan Pass farther south. Stikelan, like Cheshi, is a wide, round-bottomed, glacier-ground groove between the two big lakes. We can see facets of Mount Moore down past the low end of Tatlayoko, lying flat and iron-coloured several thousand feet below us. The mountain ridges across the lake, capped by Niut Mountain at the north end and Ottarasko in the back, sit and wait.

I have been around those mountains long enough, stared at them on the far side of the lake from Iris's cabin sufficiently, to sense that these great entities under their snow blankets are, in some stony, implacable, obdurate way, lively. Niut was known in myth time, when mountains lived, as Eniyud, and as that moody personage, that particular collection of energies with that name we humans have bestowed upon her, she had a stormy marriage with Ts'yl-os, a great lone massif overlooking Nemaiah Valley. Both mountains were known to be truculent. Eventually, after much quarrelling, so the old story goes, Eniyud stormed off over to Tatlayoko taking most of the children with her.

On the Potato Mountain ridge, looking west over Tatlayoko Lake. Photo courtesy of Chris Schreiber.

Animal tracks are everywhere, all sizes, all fresh and all over, up the hillside and down into the standing timber, but mainly on or close to the trail. There is a slightly frantic look to them, especially those of the small critters, the voles and mice, as if their late-summer food-gathering routines had been suddenly, grossly and unexpectedly interrupted. Their tracks suggest a sense of confoundedness at the disappearance of the grasses lying flattened but enticing under the snow somewhere, and their first post-snowfall efforts were simply to confirm that they were stopped from venturing farther out into the deep stuff. The details of their brief explorations into new snow are sharp down to the tiniest toe. In the dead of winter they would be holed up, food stores intact, underground.

The larger wild animals use the trail for the same reasons we and the cows do, to move up or down a steep hillside relatively easily and quickly. A good, wide, switchbacked, stock trail evens out the steepest grades and eliminates much of the sliding and skidding that is hard for even the sure-footed to avoid. A heavy mule deer buck, caught in the high country as bucks will be, has made his way downhill, hoof tracks splayed wide. Rabbits with their big snowshoe feet are obviously undeterred by this early snowfall, and their presence in numbers is clearly marked by great print sets showing leaps of a yard or more. Squirrels continue to expend energy, snow or no snow, in their endless need to drive each other out of their respective territories, racing from tree to ground to tree again, back and forth, all chases easy to read in the new white groundcover. The "chasee" in front is the one making the sharpest and most sudden turns to escape; the aggrieved territory holder behind has merely to follow, adjust and aggravate.

Halfway up, we spot several sets of bear tracks, all evidently black bears, based on the shape of the toe rows and the short claw marks, though grizzlies pass through this neck of the woods also. Most of the tracks are clear, the details just so. The first sets are of a pair of adult-sized bears walking more or less parallel to each other, ambling in a seemingly casual manner up out of the thickly timbered hillside farther east above the well-used horse trail to Bracewell's mountain cabin between the Echo Lakes. The bear tracks cross our stock trail at an open point and disappear down the near-sheer cliff faces toward Tatlayoko Lake to the west; they are obviously certain of a proven, probably ancient, route down.

What is so attractive about these print sets is that the animals seem so unhurried, so relaxed, causing me to wonder if they might be a couple in the early courting stages out on a saunter, he nosing along behind her. Or has Junior merely grown to become the same size as Mama?

The second set is farther uphill and less distinct. This bear was travelling earlier, when snow was falling, partially filling its tracks, but I can see that the animal was large, unmistakably a black bear, and had come up out of Tatlayoko Valley in the opposite direction from the bear couple down the hill. It crossed our trail, walked five or six steps past it into deeper snow and stopped. Beyond that the snow was totally unbroken. I gawk and exclaim, "Hey, Chris, these tracks don't go anywhere!" As

There is a quality about their tracks, something seemingly unimaginative and dead serious about their forthright forays out into this great white, windblown, dangerous world.

I speak, I realize that our ursine trail companion had caught him/herself, stopped and, maybe muttering something in bear self-talk like "Hold'er there, Bub, I've overshot the trail," proceeded to back up in its own footprints, turn a sharp left at the stock track and push on up the trail in front of us into more falling snow—all this approximately a day earlier. This bear character knew the route and was certain he or she was headed for the high country, perhaps aimed at the sub-alpine valley where the Echo Lakes are situated.

We follow the footsteps up to where the ridge begins to level off, checking out the small bird tracks along the way. We disturb small migrating flocks of juncos, and I recall that we had been seeing occasional moving flocks for days now; most of the bird tracks on the ground are similar to each other. On top, all over, are tracks of white-tailed ptarmigan, unmistakable, walking in straight, determined lines to wherever they were intending to go, the way ptarmigan do. Only ptarmigan have those big feathery feet to help them get around and survive in the high Arctic-like climate up here: round, quarter-sized prints placed resolutely in the snow exactly two inches apart. There is a quality about their tracks, something seemingly unimaginative and dead serious about their forthright forays out into this great white, windblown, dangerous world. Early winter is a critical business

The sound comes to us as a two-part cadence, tolling: first the blow, then the echo ...

up here and definitely not amusing. Whisky jacks ghost about close. A few Clark's nutcrackers, trying to look nonchalant, dutifully announce our passing. "Thanks, corvids, you've blatted our presence to the whole hillside yet again." They sound a bit distracted, as if something else is on their collective nutcracker-mind. A sharp-shinned hawk drops by for a quick, half-hearted harass, then flies on. A hawk's gotta do what a hawk's gotta do, and practice is so essential in these high places. The nutcrackers hardly bother to respond.

Down in the valley, some distance away but echoing up to us cleanly in the still, cool air, somebody at Bracewell's, son Alex probably, is hammering: slow, heavy, sledge-steel on steel, banging hard. The sound comes to us as a two-part cadence, tolling: first the blow, then the echo ... the blow, then the echo ... The snow on the hillsides and in the valley, and the stillness itself, absorbs and deadens further reverberation; that hammer sound, nearly visible, seems to hang in space. A passing raven, not so high, spotting the moving Gore-Tex in the usual unnaturally bright colours, slows and circles to see who or what we are down there in the

44

perfect white, then calls out in the predictable raven manner. Its call is a near-flawless imitation of the hammer blow, right down to the metallic tone deep in the throat, and the echo after-beat, muffled, edgeless. Raven likes it and tries it again and, after a pause, again, fine-tuning the nuances with the same slow cadence as that backcountry metal-banger down in the valley below us. And it seems to me now, as I recollect, that I may have heard a note of self-congratulation, a hint of a hollow chuckle, in the bird's sound-shifter tones. Time does deepen memory, and ravens do so often appear pleased with themselves. The bird flies off, slow-winged and sure and black against the Nemaiah Mountains across Chilko Lake. He wings over the low rise of Cheshi Pass and disappears down the long slope on the eastern side: blackness diminishing to nothingness.

Alex's father, Alf, patriarch to the Bracewell clan, died just a few weeks earlier, another Chilcotin legend passed on through.

The sun is thin but shining through the cloud cover. This small corner of the Potato Mountains in Tatlayoko land ("Chunazch'ez" on some of the more recent maps) is brightening up. But for occasional drifting fog patches, we are able to see most of the closer mountains, a wide sweep of summits and ridges ranging from far to the southeast to the north end of Tatlayoko Lake behind us. I discern where the Homathko River drops and cuts sharply through the core of the Coast Range to the southwest in front of us, and see steep, snow-covered glaciers hanging high off the more shadowed peaks. We sit on a pair of snow-free, windblown rocks for lunch, wordless as we munch and gaze and ponder, until one of us, me as I recall, exalts, "Damn, it's beautiful up here."

Late that afternoon, on our way back up the lake, Chris and I come upon the major part of the cow herd bunched up not far from Iris and Dennis's place. They've been pushed along the road right-of-way by Les and Colleen Harris, and a helper, in pickups. Colleen, with her toy dog under one arm—to stop him from cow chasing, I guess—was running about, dropping off salt blocks to keep the cattle from wandering away that night. Life carries on in Tatlayoko Valley.

THE VIEW SOUTH FROM THE

TATLA LAKE CEMETERY

To climb those coming crests
one word to you, to
you and your children:
Stay together
learn the flowers
go light

"For the Children"
—Gary Snyder

I HAVE BEEN through parts of this West Chilcotin country often since the early eighties, and occasionally in recent years, usually in spring, I have taken the short, slightly circuitous sidetrack to the cemetery on the ridge edge overlooking the community of Tatla Lake. The aspect of this place is approximately south, toward the sun; on a clear day, the view out to the beginning of the beyond is staggering.

Before our short walk in the Potato Mountains above Tatlayoko Lake, Chris and I were up here to take pictures. While he is organizing his camera equipment, I lean on the rail fence across the front of the cemetery and recall my first connections here and the people in these valleys, alive and dead, many buried in this place.

The Graham family's stoutly wired fenced plot is to my immediate right; the offspring lie in a neat row to one side. The Grahams were the primary proprietors of the ranch below and are the only family group up here with their own metal fence, in stark contrast to the other folks interred around them. The rest of the gravestones and graves—some simply unmarked depressions in the ground—and faded clumps of plastic flowers are scattered across the open, pine-treed slope behind me.

I brace one foot on a low fence log and lean in for a good scan of the whole wide panorama in front of me.

I can see everything. To my left, the corrals and hayfields of the Tatla Lake Ranch stretch east toward the lake, out of sight around the corner; in front are various outbuildings, a couple of dwellings and the famous old Graham ranch house inn. Dave Wright's West Chilcotin Trading Ltd., plus post office and car garage (otherwise called "the store"), sits across the yard to the right, and busy duck ponds and sloughs lie in behind. The rest of the small community is dispersed along the road west toward Kleena Kleene, Towdystan, Nimpo Lake and other such places. The highway to points east bisects the fields, and two routes run south off that road: the relatively new gravelled mainline to Tatlayoko Lake and, branching southwest by a small alkaline pond just out of Tatla, the old track to West Branch. On maps, West Branch is referred to as Mosley Creek.

In the back of the viewscape, the gap in the mountains that is West Branch drops away to the southwest down the steep defile of Mosley Creek. Razorback, Blackhorn and Whitesaddle mountains, the Niut Range, with Ottarasko capping it off at the back, all snow- and ice-capped, all imposing, stand on the east side. The course of the valley itself curls out of sight.

Farther to the east there is only a low gap in the plateau skyline, a blank, a negative space, to indicate the existence of Tatlayoko Lake and its artery, the Homathko River, which flows south and southwest. The lake is surrounded by mountains in every direction but north and northeast, and they are every bit as impressive as those around West Branch, but many more miles farther south. A near infinity of Coast Range peaks, most hidden, lies beyond. Somewhere down there on the river is Murderer's

A portion of the community of Tatla Lake as seen from the cemetery. The old Graham Ranch house is in the centre. Photo courtesy of Chris Schreiber.

Bar, the major, but not sole, site of the Chilcotin War in 1864. Mosley Creek joins the Homathko not far above that surely haunted killing site. The river reaches sea level at the head of Bute Inlet.

The east, or main, branch of the Homathko River rises in swamps and mountain edges a few miles south of Tatla. Mosley Creek begins not far west, at Little Sapeye Lake and the hillsides close by. Hook Lake, a mile or so to the southwest, drains in the opposite direction into Tatla Creek and Tatla Lake and, eventually, the Chilcotin River, which runs to the Fraser. The divide through there is difficult to spot unless you are searching for it. Overall, the divide between the Chilcotin River drainages to the north and east and the southward flow of the two branches of the Homathko into Bute, plus the westward flows of the Klinaklini and other rivers into inlets farther north, meanders from slough to slough here and there across the northwest Chilcotin. The phenomenon of that invisible, wandering divide, all of it well east of the mountaintops, and the series of fast rivers plunging down through the wide Coast Range from its back side to its front, is one of the wonders of the region.

This area around Tatla has always been a crossroads, now and in the old days. There are resonances of history here.

This area around Tatla has always been a crossroads, now and in the old days. There are resonances of history here, perhaps none more provoking than the stories of Chiwid, who in the early years of the twentieth century, after a serious beating from her husband, took to the woods and wandered back and forth across the Chilcotin Plateau according to the season, living off it for the rest of her long, wild life. How she survived those Chilcotin winters is another true wonder. She would have passed through Tatla Lake many times in her comings and goings. Betty Linder (later MacDonald), the storekeeper and daughter of ranch owner Bob Graham, lived here, and Betty and her husband, Fred, took it upon themselves to help Chiwid and keep an eye on her through her elder years. I wonder if the little cabin they set up as a shelter for her in the cold months still stands, and, if so, which building down there in front of me it would be. Apparently Chiwid chose not to use it much; she found it too cold, as she did all houses in winter no matter how hot the fire burned. She felt more comfortable outside.

Chiwid's spirit cuts through this place like a sharp-edged knife. At the beginning of *Chiwid,* Sage Birchwater's fine book about her, there is a quote from Marty Moore, grandson of Tatlayoko pioneer Ken Moore, who told Sage: "One time in late fall, people were hearing strange noises above Tatla Lake, and people called in the authorities ... The locals were laughing about it. All they ever found was old Chiwid's camp. It sounded like a cougar screaming or a wolf howling, they said." That story still raises the hairs on my neck.

Chiwid's camp would have been somewhere close to this graveyard looking out over the flats, where lie Edgar Hamm, Hilda and Leonard Butler, Clarence MacKill, Baptiste Dester, Tom Chignell, Bob and Margaret Graham and their sons Bill and Alex, Betty (Linder) MacDonald, Fred Linder and all the rest—a host of worthy, and perhaps a few not so worthy, colonists from more settled, more "civilized" parts of the world, and some of their descendants, the ones who stayed. Death doesn't care much about "worthy." There are stories drifting around about them all.

The air continues clear, the sky deep blue, the mountains are all glistening, and the light of the heavens reflects silver off the lakes and sloughs and winding watercourses.

Chiwid, wandering woman of the Chilcotin.
Photo courtesy of Veera Bonner.

Sarah Schuk, mother of Joe and Ed and seven other children, is buried here also, right next to Lloyd McGhee, both just a short distance upslope from the Graham plot. Sarah lived long, worked hard and died in 1986 having, with husband Martin, uprooted and traversed half a continent, half a century earlier, to get here. She lived a life out in these western mountains in this new and untamed place, this "great lone land," far from the flat prairies of her young years. Ensconced close by beside Lloyd is his older brother, Harry McGhee, who is connected to the Schuks by marriage.

Ultimately, nearly everyone here is related, closely or distantly, to nearly everyone else in the Chilcotin, and now some of those old ones lie up there behind me in their little rows and groups, resting and warming their bones in the dry, sunny, sloped earth enclosed around them, keeping them safe.

Two days after our most recent arrival here, Joe Schuk and I stood on the porch outside the store for a few minutes, chatting and watching the snow fall. Chris and I were in to fix a slow flat on the Pathfinder—caused by a pair of nails, still stuck in the tire it turns out, that I'd picked up probably in Lee Butler's yard down in West Branch that morning. I'd been over to talk with Lee some more, getting details and flavours for a story I'm working on, and enjoying his precise responses and clear, modest presence. Joe, who lived in West Branch when he first came here, later moving over to Tatlayoko to become a successful rancher in his own right, asked in that powerful gravelly voice of his, "You boys just come into this country?"

He went on to speak of making a living here and how this country was more than just a pretty place. He told a little story of the tourist lady who bemoaned the new power poles put in about 1980 to bring power and some amenities of modern living into the valleys. She saw them as eyesores marring the picturesque, seemingly idyllic qualities of the land. Joe said, and it was the second time I'd heard him say it, "People say how beautiful this country is, but I say a feast for the eyes don't keep the big guts from eating the short guts." In other words, this was a tough country and still is; the illusion of comfort is in short supply, and the dynamics of life and death are real and upfront out here.

That evening, as we cooked supper, Chris remarked on Joe's classic Chilcotin salutation in the afternoon. I recalled the moment with a little inward smile and thought that, compared to Joe Schuk, I was a rank newcomer, a mere pensioner and relatively young. Joe was an amazingly tough eighty-seven years old at that time and had lived here all his adult life.

I had just reintroduced myself to him and his wife, Katie, in the store, where they were sitting, enjoying a hot cup of coffee. He remembered I'd spent time with them the previous spring in the kitchen of their ranch house by Crazy Creek down in Tatlayoko, talking about history and the world of ranching and survival in the Chilcotin, and now he came outside to talk for a few minutes. Joe is a strongly built man of medium height who stands with both feet square on the ground and speaks with all the authority of one who has lived, worked and succeeded in this hard country. I appreciated their courtesy.

Joe was waiting for Katie to finish up in the store. As we stood there, his brother Ed drove up through the sleet with his wife, Helen, from their place over at Lunch Lake, on the old Tatlayoko cutoff road, in a fairly new, small, four-by-four vehicle similar to the one Joe was driving. I had not had the privilege of meeting them before but recognized them from articles and pictures in *Hoofprints in History*, a fine series of biographies

Joe and Katie Schuk with Helen and Ed Schuk at "the lower place." Photo courtesy of Joe and Katie Schuk.

of local Chilcotin old-timers, compiled over the years by Tatla Lake Junior High School students. Helen was known to be especially history-minded. Joe and Katie, Helen's sister, were also interviewed for *Hoofprints*. In their article, they take us on an old-time cattle drive (one of the last) across country and the Fraser River to the stockyards at Williams Lake.

Helen and Ed Schuk have since passed away, Helen first and Ed a few months later.

Katie and Helen are the daughters of Harry and Amelia McGhee, themselves among the first settlers, after Ken Moore and a few others, to homestead in the Tatlayoko Valley. The McGhees arrived in the valley in 1925, having come all the long way from Nebraska. They stopped at Horsefly first, then moved on across the Fraser River to the Tatla Lake region where, as new settlers seemed often to do, Katie noted that "the grass came up to a horse's belly." Such fecundity is a sure and time-honoured sign that you have arrived, and the McGhees stopped to stay and put down roots. The roads out here were just tracks in those days. They first settled down-valley above Moore's, close to the head of the lake, where the local climate allowed them to maintain a big kitchen garden and small, hardy orchard. Later they bought Charlie Parks's place at the upper end of the Tatlayoko Valley, moving between both places according to the demands of the seasons. The McGhees ranged their cattle down at Stikelan Pass until wolves forced them to seek new range up in the Potato Mountains. Both McGhee sisters were born in the Chilcotin: Helen at the Red Cross Outpost Hospital at Alexis Creek and Katie at Moore's ranch in Tatlayoko.

Their lower place came eventually to be owned by Ken Hesch and, like the Moore ranch nearby and Skinner Meadow off the road to Big Eagle (Choelquoit) Lake, is now owned by the Nature Conservancy of Canada, a development that is not without consequence and controversy. These days, there are differences of opinion in Tatlayoko as to whether such long-distance ownership is good for the local community and economy. Whatever the benefits to local wildlife may be, "no trespassing" signs and locked gates have become more common and serve to stop travellers, including descendants of the original inhabitants, from using some old trails, roads and country in the long-accustomed way. There is a sense that these former ranch properties have become the recreational preserve of the urban affluent. Certainly the local population is reduced, and the Nature Conservancy purchases seem to reinforce the decline of ranching in the valley.

Joe Schuk himself "came into the country" in 1936 in a 1928 Plymouth sedan with his grandparents Dave and Sarah Hamm and part of their family—Bert, Dave Jr., Edgar and Wanda—exiles all from the depressed and dusty conditions of the "dirty thirties" around Rosthern, Saskatchewan. Although there was scant extra room in the crowded vehicle, the eager young Joe persuaded his relatives to squeeze him in and take him along. The Hamms, from a family-conscious, Mennonite background, were reluctant to refuse him. This group had been preceded in 1932 by an older Hamm brother, Johnny; his two sisters, Annie and Tildy; and their respective husbands, Bob Nicholson and Charlie Godfrey, all hoping to start a new life somewhere in the British Columbia Interior. Apparently the three brothers-in-law bumped into the infamous Theodore Valleau in a Williams Lake hotel where, so the story goes, he persuaded the new immigrants to cross the wide Chilcotin Plateau and check out where he lived at West Branch in the mountains south of Tatla Lake. Valleau was normally known to be reclusive, defensive and vigorously hostile to newcomers to his home valley, so the Johnny Hamm party caught him on an unusually good day.

Joe Schuk, Bert and Edgar Hamm, the senior Hamms, and Annie Nicholson and her five children remained in the area; others moved away or died. Annie Nicholson's story of survival down there at the bottom end of West Branch is a small epic all by itself, as we shall see in the next chapter.

When he realized that the amount of good and available growing and cattle-rearing land down in West Branch was limited, Joe, who was clearly ambitious, hard-working and quite capable of earning and saving a grubstake, even in this difficult land in those difficult times, bought the Bellamy ranch over in Tatlayoko in 1942. Earlier, he had invited his parents, Martin and Sarah, to come out and join him. Tatlayoko–West Branch must have seemed to these immigrants from Saskatchewan like some vale of Eden: strange, tough, isolated, enclosed and dark in winter no doubt, but still a little like paradise, especially on a warm sunny morning in the spring of the year when much of the region was still seized with cold. Here they found not only available land but also, in contrast to the dried-out, sunburnt land from whence they came, plenty of water and

Farm machinery at the Schuk Ranch by Crazy Creek. Photo courtesy of John Schreiber.

wood, a substantial deer and expanding moose population to hunt, the occasional outside job for cash, and an adequate growing climate in the valley bottoms. Above all, they found hope; all they had to do was endure and work, constantly and hard, and stick together.

Unlike much of the rest of the Chilcotin, West Branch and Tatlayoko Valley are, relatively speaking, something of a "banana belt." The two valleys lie roughly parallel to each other on the edge of the plateau, and are lower in elevation. They are both exposed, to the south and southwest, not only to the sun, but also, when the winds are blowing right, to warm, moisture-bearing, coast air coming up from Bute Inlet. In spring and summer, the valleys are warmed by the accumulating heat of the Interior east of the mountains. This warmth combines with their lower elevations to make these valleys Douglas fir zones; the diversity of plant life is richer than in the lodgepole pine forests and spruce swamps up on the western plateau. In the Tatlayoko Valley, the climate is moderated by the waters of Tatlayoko Lake, and by cooling winds funneling up the lake off the snowy mountains and glaciers most summer afternoons. The series of smaller lakes at the top end of the Mosley Creek valley have a similar effect in West Branch, and those breezes blow the bugs away, at least for a while.

I first met Joe and Katie Schuk at Iris Moore and Dennis Redford's place in 2002. The encounter was short. It was a fine sunny September afternoon, and I had just come down off the south route to the top of Potato Mountain ridge. I'd been up there above tree line, examining bear cub tracks in the dry earth and walking with the mountain gods, or so it felt. That was my first time up the south end, and I was enthusiastic about the wide, switchbacked, stock trail, first cut and dug, incidentally, by Harry McGhee, up the 4,000 feet of steep, open, potentially difficult hillside. Joe struck me immediately as a man of strength and presence, despite his then recent bout with cancer. I had the feeling that he was pleased to hear something positive, however limited, about cow trails in the alpine.

In the spring of '06, when I phoned the Schuk residence to set up a time to talk, Katie said, "Well, Joe will be out irrigating in the morning." Joe hadn't become the biggest rancher in the district by lying around; the habits of a lifetime of work persist. Over those decades, Joe has run his cows up on Crazy Creek Mountain, in the Potato Mountains, and over on the other side of the Chilko River around Eagle Lake Henry's old place, where Joe's son Clifford and family now reside. He quit the Crazy Creek range when a bear, probably a grizzly, started "eating all his cows." He and Katie had owned Skinner Meadow for its hay crop and as a handy site to feed cattle in winter.

I arrived after lunchtime to find Katie and Joe, still in from irrigating his hayfields, accompanied by a neighbour, George Meilleur, who had been working with Joe. George was from the Crazy Creek Ranch just down the road. I explained that I was writing about the West Chilcotin country, old-timers and history, and started asking a few introductory questions. I quickly learned some of the basic facts of ranch life around Crazy Creek—for example, that Joe and Katie built their present home in 1955. Joe talked of the difficulty of bringing in large panes of glass in those road-poor years, and commented that glass made for a cold house. "I can tell you that life is a lot better with electricity," Joe said. "It was hard to live down here in the old days." Some ranchers took out guiding licences to augment their income, but guide-outfitting took too much time away from the daily routines of ranching. Trapping was more convenient.

It wasn't too long before we were talking of some of the old West Chilcotin characters like Charlie Skinner, father of Chiwid (Lily Skinner), and Frank Render, the expert log-house builder from Kleena Kleene who worked on Skinner's roadhouse, built a century earlier in anticipation of the railroad from Bute Inlet that never came. That particular edifice was only half completed, but it was solidly built and still stands on the edge of the expansive meadow named after Charlie. It was Ken Moore who ditched and drained Skinner Meadow to turn it into a productive hayfield. Eagle Lake Henry's name came up briefly. Mary Jane Lulua's name was mentioned. She was the youngest daughter of Chiwid, and her childhood must have been tough, tagging along behind her wild mother as they meandered across the country. Other characters were discussed—Arlee Holt; Billy Dagg; Sam Colwell; Old Man Schilling, first rancher at Anahim Lake; Bert Lehman; Fred Engbretson, the "mayor" of Towdystan; and Purjue (which of the several Purjue brothers, I wasn't certain, but I assume it was Will, who had lived down in Tatlayoko)—and place names like Gordon meadow, Henry's meadow, Captain Lloyd's meadow, Fishtrap Lake, Canoe Crossing over by Chilko Lake, the Three Circle Ranch, and apple trees down the Klinaklini River. All fascinating, all topics too quickly raised and dropped, all names I knew bits about, but only enough to thoroughly whet my curiosity more and drive me ever so slightly crazy.

Charlie Skinner's unfinished roadhouse at Skinner Meadow. Photo courtesy of Marne St. Claire.

My usual practice in these get-togethers, born of a desire to be unobtrusive, is to let the talk go where it will, but here I wish that I'd slowed the conversation a little and dug into the details of just a few of those amazing folks, whom storytelling and mythologizing have turned into small-scale legends. These were ordinary people, wild places, tough times, extraordinary circumstances, with few of the moderating influences of society at large, and small myth-stories have emerged and are emerging now. And these are just a few of the characters and instances; such discussions are only ever a start.

> *Supposedly he was on the run from the Dalton Gang of train robbers down in the United States.*

Naturally, the subject of George Turner from Kleena Kleene came up; it usually does out here sooner or later, and there was considerable talk about him. Supposedly he was on the run from the Dalton Gang of train robbers down in the United States. That's what people say, but experiences vary and opinions differ widely as to the actual truth of many of the old stories about him. It was agreed that there were "good, hard-working Indians" back in Turner's day; Thomas Squinas from up at Anahim was mentioned as one of a number of such examples. "Those old guys could sure build good fences," Joe said. "Those fences Billy Dagg built still stand."

Somebody referred to Katie and Helen's uncle Lloyd McGhee, who, I hadn't realized, had started what is now called the Peterson Place, past the far end of Skinner Meadow on the old track to Big Eagle Lake and the Chilko River. The barn still stands, as does the original house-turned-chicken coop; the newer house is more elaborate and still intact, though increasingly weather-worn. There have been a succession of owners, and the stories circling around one of them are sufficiently bizarre to acquire a kind of underground currency; local people seem not to offer details readily.

I recalled that my friend Peter Stein and I had walked down to the Peterson Place one cool bright autumn day some years back and, on our return, heard wolves howling in the woods on the low divide southwest of the meadow. Joe's cattle stopped their feeding instantly and began to trot away from the forest edges, the cows calmly leading their calves out as if all this was routine business. Even the bulls lumbered out. They gathered in scattered groups at the centre of the meadow, with only a minimum of bawling, and carried right on with their grazing and chewing. It was difficult to be sure how close, or far away, the wolves were; their sound was clear, without echo and somewhat directionless out there in those thick woods and still air.

Then we got to talking about Pan Phillips and Rich Hobson, author of *Grass beyond the Mountains*. I said I had reread that book not too long before and, suspecting Rich and Pan were capable of at least a little BS—Pan in the telling, Rich in the writing—read it the second time with the maps out to check the distances quoted. I reported that Rich had exaggerated the distances of their epic cattle drive over the Ilgachuz and Itcha mountain ranges to their home ranch site up near Stuyvesant Lake by a consistent 60 percent, give or take a few points. This led to a pithy discussion as to the nature of bullshit, with Joe suggesting there was a necessary distinction between "good bullshit" and "bad bullshit."

This was not the first time I'd discussed that particular nuance—I'd heard coast loggers make a similar distinction back in my bunkhouse days. Joe has a good point. Generally, if a story is well told, with lots of pertinent detail, it's "good bullshit." The difference is not necessarily sharp, and it definitely varies according to the teller, but under the circumstances, we concurred that Rich's stories, being well-intended and time-tested, were "good bullshit," whereas a bald-faced lie is likely "bad bullshit." Some bullshitters are incapable of anything but bad bullshit. Gossip is not good bullshit, especially as it's so often negative and hurtful. I suspect, over time, much good bullshit merges into myth. It is important to re-clarify these distinctions occasionally.

Somehow, in all this discussion, someone happened to mention the topic of cattle. Joe told a story of the time when Rose Meilleur, relatively new to the country, asked Calvin Schuk how many cattle he had. "Enough," said Calvin in a gruff voice. Everyone chuckled, and another good local story inched closer to legend.

"A rancher never lies till you ask him how many cows he's got," Joe explained. I gather you never inquire, except in the most general of terms, about cattle in ranch country. It's like asking a person how much land they own or how much money they make. We talked about haying, and Joe said, "Of course, if you've got a crop at all, it's a good crop."

He suggested Katie get out the cookies to go with the coffee. She did, but not much later, despite a flood of questions in my head, my manners kicked in. We were talking about land prices, always a dicey topic. I suspected Joe wanted to get on with laying pipe, so I felt I should begin to wrap things up, but first I asked George Meilleur how he managed to come to this Tatlayoko country. He replied that the mountains, the availability of land and the sense of community lured him. It turned out we both knew Warren Menhinick, the guide-outfitter and horseman out of Gold Bridge. We agreed that Warren was a complete cowboy and outdoorsman, and a good man to ride with in the backcountry. George was from down around Whistler and not much impressed with what his old haunts had come to in these modern times.

These are smart, capable, hospitable people. Their home was plain, and Katie and Joe were warm and welcoming. Katie has a winning smile, and her face lit up when I told her I'd send them a copy of the finished story to check when it was done. She also has a sly humour; in the discussions back and forth, I could see her dancing the practised dance of a lifetime, lightly moving around, and by and with, her bull-of-the-woods husband, Joe Schuk, the alpha rancher of Tatlayoko Valley. I believe my broad, but not deep, aware-

I could see her dancing the practised dance of a lifetime, lightly moving around, and by and with, her bull-of-the-woods husband.

ness of their country helped the discourse, and I presume they could see my interest in their way of life up here as a statement of honest acknowledgement and respect. I hope they enjoyed the visit as much as I did, and I looked forward to seeing them again. Of course I had more questions.

In May of the following year, I did see Joe and Katie again, as a courtesy to them and to make any necessary corrections to this story. Winter had been difficult, with much snow and rain followed by deep cold. Everything froze hard, then more snow fell. It was easy to get stuck and difficult to get out. I had the feeling Joe and Katie were a bit overawed by the duration of it all and, not surprisingly, were glad to see the start of spring. I had heard that Katie had medical problems of a possibly serious nature, and my visit had a slightly sombre quality about it. The Schuks were gracious as usual.

Among other topics, we talked about riding and walking. I asked Katie if she had gotten to be a good rider when she was young. She said, with what I suspect is characteristic modesty, "Not really, not so people would notice."

"Did you like to ride?" I asked.

"Oh yeah, I did," she replied.

"It was the only way we got around in the early days," Joe said, "besides walking. I'd walk up to Tatla to the store, and then maybe down to Kleena Kleene, all in a day."

That would have been along the old road by Graveyard Springs, I thought.

"I walked fifty miles one time, back in Saskatchewan," Joe said. "Took me seventeen hours, but I was too proud to hitch."

"Holy smokes," I retorted in awe. The most miles I had ever knowingly covered in one day was eighteen, and I fancy myself a walker. Mind you, up-and-down bush miles are longer and tougher than straight-road prairie miles.

Joe remarked that when you irrigate and pack all that pipe, you walk a lot. "But," he said, "my walking days are over, my riding days are over. But it would be good to ride; sometimes the work needs an hour on a horse." He still had three horses, two younger ones and an old saddle mare who decided one day she wasn't going to work anymore. She'd had enough. "She was a good horse; who says horses aren't smart?"

I asked Joe if he'd taken cattle up the trail above the old mill site recently to summer range in the Potatoes. I had just been up there and had seen no new cow tracks or poop piles from the previous summer.

"Well," he said, not so obliquely, "there are people from far away who are opposed to cattle in the alpine country, as if it's any of their business." Joe looked right at me. "Do you know any of those kinds of people?" He went on to say that it was good to drive the herd up into high summer range to get them away from the timber milk vetch. This member of the pea family, cousin to locoweed, is dangerous to lactating cows when its sap is milky. When cattle eat it, they hit their heels as they walk, swell up lopsided, lose their voice and their ability to digest, and die. Joe said he cut one such cow carcass open and found nothing in the lower intestine but sand.

I told him I'd followed bear tracks up the trail that morning: a small grizzly on the heels of a black bear mother and her young cub. I spotted the cub's tiny toes in tight little rows in snow patches, all fresh, judging by the rapid deterioration of my own half-melted footprints on my way back down. The animal tracks must have been just hours old. On the way up, black mama meandered somewhat, but the grizzly's path was straight and clearly purposeful. The adult bears veered off into thick timber just below tree line. But there was a sizable patch on a shadowed snowbank where mama black bear had stomped around repeatedly as if she was agitated. Her footprints suggested she'd been turning; her feet were still muddy from the wet dirt trail downhill. Had she been waiting for her wandering young one maybe, or was the grizzly behind too close for comfort, forcing her to stand, be fierce, look big and defend? I could not find the cub's prints. Had mother bear driven it up a tree for safety?

"They say grizzlies are going extinct, but sure as hell not around here," Joe said. "We had a grizzly in the yard just the other day. But there are fewer black bears." There always are when griz move into the neighbourhood. To them, a small black bear, unaccompanied by a tough mum, is meat. Grizzlies are the reason black bears developed their covert survival habits across most of the continent.

I asked about the rest of the big game species. Cougars are not much bother, nor wolves especially; light winters have been good for the deer population, but moose numbers are down, due to all the additional logging road access for hunters these years.

Out of the blue, Joe asked if I had ever met Cyril Shelford from up in the Ootsa Lake country. I said no, but I had read a book he wrote about homesteading up there and thought he sounded like an interesting man. Shelford had been Minister of Agriculture under W.A.C. Bennett. Joe must be an old-time Socred, I'm guessing. It would fit.

All the time we were talking, Katie was cleaning up around the stove, taking it apart and scrubbing the burner sections where Joe let the rice boil over when he was batching while she was away at Williams Lake having her tests done. "You know how rice sticks." She would join in to correct a point or comment, then carry on cleaning. She looked tired. Joe said he had missed her cooking. The feeling of our meeting got a bit sober at this point, and I thought it was about time to take my leave.

Once again, Katie and Joe struck me as tough, brave, unsentimental and hospitable, but the current dilemma seemed to be wearing them down, and there was poignancy in the situation. Joe closed his eyes and screwed up his face when he talked, taking his time between utterances to compose his thoughts and not forget. I sat silent and waited, knowing his comments would be well-considered and clearly delivered.

I stood up and Joe rose to see me out. He stands shorter than me, but his shoulders are massively broad, and he has a resolute quality about him. They said, "Drop in if you're by," more polite than heartfelt, but I appreciated it. At the door, I said to Katie that I had heard she had medical issues and asked how things were going. She shrugged.

"I hope all goes well," I said.

"So do I," she replied with a little smile, a quick life-light in her blue eyes. I left feeling tired and slightly desolate. It is too easy to say aging is just nature's way.

Joe Schuk's ninetieth birthday celebration, 2008. Photo courtesy of Joe and Katie Schuk.

By any measure, I am an elder: I was born in 1941, I collect a pension and I remember talk of the "Adam" bomb in 1945. But five years before I came into this world, Joe Schuk was working and making a living for himself, probably with an eye to ranching, over in West Branch. Two pictures taken in 1936, and included in an autobiography self-published by long-time West Branch resident Bert Hamm, show Joe doing exactly that: working and, from the looks of it, putting his broad back whole-heartedly into the sawmilling job at hand. Seventy-plus years later, he is still here in Tatlayoko Valley, still irrigating, still working the ranching life, and I doubt he would have had it any other way. I cannot imagine him or Katie complaining about it. This is what I admire about so many of these old-timers up here in this most pragmatic, non-urban corner of this province.

Joe Schuk and I were standing outside the store; the snow, more like sleet now, was still coming down. We had been talking, briefly, about getting older, a perennial topic these days it seems. Joe said, "The years are really going by fast now." I nodded. He looked at me and stated, in tones of mild regret, genuinely felt I'm sure, "I didn't butcher last year; it's hard. You know, I can't lift a quarter of beef anymore." But the look passing on his face was also of subtle pride. And I read his statement as "But I could do it, and I did it and a thousand jobs like it my whole life."

Katie comes out from the store slowly; she is partially bent over with arthritis. But she flashes that smile, the same smile I saw in the spring at their place, the same charming smile captured in a photo with the Schuks' story in *Hoofprints in History*, when she was a young mother with her apron on, attractive, with her babe in her arms. It's right above another of her and Joe, years later, standing together and cutting their anniversary cake. There is a look in that second picture, just a hint, of triumph on her face.

WILD LIFE IN THE WEST BRANCH:

ANNIE NICHOLSON

What is life?
It is the flash of a firefly in the night.
It is the breath of a buffalo in the winter time.
It is the little shadow which runs across the grass
and loses itself in the sunset.

—Crowfoot, Blackfoot elder and chief, in his dying hours
April 1890

I TOOK THE old route down into West Branch one sunny day in June. This is the narrow, grown-in track that branches off the main road just south of Tatla Lake and runs to the southwest by Hook and Little Sapeye lakes. In earlier times, Young Guichon had a cabin in a meadow over there, close to the little watercourse flowing out of the swamps into Hook Lake. I'm guessing that his father, Old Guichon, lived in that same place before him, and Chiwid used to camp there. Any time I am where I know that wandering woman has been, I think of Gerry Bracewell's words in the front of Sage Birchwater's book about her, a remembrance with a touch of myth in it that has left its mark on me: "Chiwid was a very beautiful woman when I first came into this country in 1940. I remember seeing her camped in a little grove of poplar trees at Graveyard Springs, along the old road into the West Branch. I remember how beautiful she was. All by herself, with very beautiful, long, black hair, as shiny as a raven's wing. She was just there in the wilderness."

Late afternoon, I stopped the car in the meadow just short of the creek crossing near the springs and listened. All I could hear were the usual late-in-the-day breezes whispering through pine-tree tops and last year's tall grasses. The meadow had that sense of forever about it. Then, sure enough, after a minute or two I heard the far-off, hollow honking of a sandhill crane out in the middle of the swamp. I held my breath to listen and watch. There seemed to be something moving, just barely, at the edge of my seeing: intimations, hints, of something creeping furtively through the swamp birch across my line of vision to the right. My view was to the south; the June sky was bright. More motion showed in gaps between shrubs, increasingly evident now, and I realized it was another sandhill, all hunched down, neck folded, skulking through the brush in the direction of that distant caller, its mate I have no doubt.

I sidled slowly across behind a tall saskatoon clump but lost sight of the skulker, who must have reached his partner. Minutes later, both birds rose calling from the centre of the swamp and slow-winged their way west to land together on a low grassy esker a couple of hundred yards beyond me, farther to my right. I had just gotten a clear focus on them in my binocs when the pair turned and stalked, methodically, away from each other. One, the bird closest to the swamp, suddenly stood up tall, arched and crooked her neck and ducked down out of sight as quick as a wink, a clearly deliberate strategy. The second bird (why do I assume it was the male?) proceeded to put on a show of what must have been decoy behaviour, flapping his wings casually and prancing along the esker away from the slough toward the high point of the rise, where he stopped and turned and waited. After a few minutes his mate called from out in the middle. He cocked his head and, uttering little honking noises, took a running jump to rise and fly off with heavy wingbeats to join her, sounding only mildly perturbed. The entire ritual had a sense of routine, a feeling almost of world-weariness about it, as if they'd done it all before and would do it again if pushed. She rose up to meet him, and the two cranes flew in a wide circle together, calling occasionally in slow unison, and finally settling farther off, out of sight. I was sure their nest was not far away. Sandhill crane couples mate for life.

Sandhill crane. Photo courtesy of Damon West Photography.

The whole time I was watching, a yellowlegs, a species of mid-sized, long-legged shorebird, perched not far from me in the top of a small spruce tree, looking incongruous, the way yellowlegs in small, pointy-topped coniferous trees always do. It sounded the alarm over and over, its shrill call piercing the stillness of the swamp. An unseen killdeer, low to the ground, joined in for a few moments of half-hearted shorebird solidarity before running out of zeal, its call fading vaguely into silence.

There is something in the stately manner and rough, haunting, usually far-away call of sandhill cranes that has always fascinated me, profoundly. They are such dignified, intelligent creatures and have such an aura of antiquity and deep knowing about them. Certainly cranes, all fifteen species, most low in numbers and threatened, signify spirit and sanctity in cultures the world over. I sense that archetypical quality each time I am fortunate enough to hear or see them. I seek out these great birds for that quality. I expect I always will.

I got in my car, shifted into four-wheel high and drove through the muddy and slightly steep creek crossing. In some spindly poplars close by, about where I would have expected, I found the scant remains of a small cabin that must have been Young Guichon's, a rectangular shadow in the grass, and decayed bits of detritus: a few ancient cans, tin buckets and metal scraps, all flattened and rusting into the ground, as well as scattered fragments of rotted board. Sage Birchwater tells me that Young Guichon raised Susie Squinas, herself still alive and well at Anahim Lake. Susie is one of Thomas Squinas's daughters and was crippled from birth. Her mother, Celistine, was a Guichon, so as an infant, Susie was given to Young Guichon to bring up and keep him company. Sage mentions that there is a fine photo of Young Guichon, part of the Swannell collection, in the provincial archives.

Old Guichon was a survivor of the devastating smallpox plague that wiped out Indian people all across this country in the 1860s. He is reputed to have witnessed the ambush of the pack train at the fish trap on the Dean River near Nimpo Lake, one of several incidents in the Chilcotin War of 1864. The Tatla Lake area was his family's traditional territory.

That name, Guichon, always catches my attention because it is the name of a well-known French pioneer ranching family down in the Merritt area and around the mouth of the Fraser River. The several Guichon brothers came to British Columbia originally to join the gold rush and later were active in the pack-train business and as suppliers of merchandise to miners. Their business naturally took them into the Cariboo and probably into the Chilcotin country, likely all the way out to Bella Coola. There are or were a number of aboriginal Guichons in this West Chilcotin land, suggesting there might have been some kind of passing, old-time, "country" connection up here back then.

Apparently, after Young Guichon died, his relatives put on a little potlatch and, several years after that event, burned the old place down. He is buried nearby on the far side of the creek with other members of the Guichon family, long departed. I visited the site recently, guided by Sage's directions, and found it easily on a small bare knoll overlooking Hook Lake. There is a fairly new pine-log fence around it to keep cattle out. An old, dilapidated pile of log bits and small boards next to Young Guichon's final resting place must surely have been Old Guichon's burial site. Lee Butler believes Blind Seymour was buried there also. A few stubby poplars grow in the shade of the fence. There are similar old gravesites in lonely far-off places, often on a grassy knoll that provides a view of the land around—or perhaps a fuller, grander sense of sky—all through this country. Many such sites have neat, sometimes rickety, wooden picket fences around them, and crosses, some plain, some variously ornate.

Others are unmarked now and fading into the ground. We walk on or through them unknowing.

A short mile or so farther, the waters flow south, not northeast, to become Mosley Creek, the West Branch of the Homathko River, ultimately reaching salt water at the head of Bute Inlet. There is a shallow, white-rimmed, alkaline lake along the old road, not much more than a large pond, called Suds or Soap Lake. It is right on the divide between watersheds, without much surface flow either way, south or north. Sage, who, like me, has a thing for drainage divides, ascribes some holiness to that place and spent time alone there before his first son, Junah, was conceived.

The track south goes past Little Sapeye Lake and, below that, Waterlily Lake. There is a Forestry trail on the west side into Waterlily, improved back in those good days when the mandate of the Ministry of Forests was, in part, to facilitate public use of public lands. The trail is now cut off by high water as some cagey beavers have used the primitive footbridge across the creek there as the central component in their dam construction. Below the steep, open-wooded mountainside above Sapeye Creek, at the far end of Waterlily, is a small campsite, not new or much used. Lee Butler

Guichon graves alone in the bush at Graveyard Springs. Photo courtesy of John Schreiber.

has mentioned that Donald Ekks and Emily Lulua Ekks—and various other family members, no doubt—used to camp along these lakes in earlier days. I have noticed that Forestry campsites in the BC Interior were frequently set up at traditional camping locations, many of considerable antiquity, often by old trail or river crossings, creek outlets and hay meadows.

Somewhere close to Waterlily Lake is a route to the ridge above it, and I have an inclination to walk up it into the sub-alpine sometime soon, maybe late next spring (while I still can). It should be only a couple of thousand feet of up before the ground starts to level off; by then I would expect to be in semi-open parkland. I asked Lee if there was a trail up there. He said not—"It's just open woods on the way up"—but the quick look on his face, his eyebrows slightly raised, asked, "Why would you need one?"

Trails, of course, make walking much easier and more definitive; on a trail we are reasonably certain of where we are going. They have flow. On a trail, we walk in the wake of the trail makers, in their slipstream as it were. Trails give us legitimacy, as if by their existence we belong there. Animals, wild and domestic, are happy to use the trails we establish and keep open, many of which happened to be game trails before we two-leggeds showed up, although such pre-human walkways have the unfortunate habit, usually, of petering out suddenly just as we become used to them. I have an impression that some animals view trails as shared territory, similar to the way they view water holes in water-short regions. But life off trails, into the woods and up the mountainsides, gets wild for us humans. This land becomes their land; now we are walking in their backyard. We find ourselves slipping a few notches closer to the howlingly inchoate and the abjectly indefinable. My humility quotient and my vigilance tend to increase sharply when I'm off trail, alone in the bush. So

Donald Ekks, Emily Lulua Ekks and members of their
family. Photo courtesy of Sage Birchwater.

does my sense of being truly alive. Alone in the wild, I have learned, like most woodspeople, to experience thoroughly the meaning of awe.

It may be that our chances of finding and staying on our soul path in life increase when we step off the trail into the bush. It may be then that we slow down enough, go quiet enough, to hear the world around us and ourselves in it, so that we learn who or what we are, where we are going and to whom or what we answer. Zen poet Gary Snyder says, in *The Practice of the Wild*, "'Off the trail' is another name for the Way, and sauntering off the trail is the practice of the wild. That is where, paradoxically, we do our best work. But we need paths and trails and will always be maintaining them. You must first be on the path, before you can turn and walk into the wild."

Below Big Sapeye and Horn lakes, on the edge of a wide flat between Butler and Horn creeks, close to where they flow into the main Mosley Creek drainage, Lee and Bev Butler live. Their little ranch has a well-settled quality about it, as if people have lived there and worked it in for a while. Lee's father, Leonard, came up here from the United States with his mother, Ada, her husband, Jim Holt, and a herd of horses in the 1920s. Len married Hilda MacKill, daughter of Jim and Annie MacKill of One Eye Lake. Lee, who was born at Alexis Creek, and his brother and sister, Jack and Eleanor, are their children. Lee and Bev married in 1957 and have children and grandchildren of their own around the area.

A short distance beyond their ranch is Bluff Lake. Until the early fifties, when a road was blasted around the bluffs at lake level, this was where the wagon road stopped. From there on, all traffic into lower West Branch walked and packed on foot or by horse. Or somebody borrowed or built a boat. A trail winds its way up over the rocky open hump and down again; some of the high rock ledges look as if they had been widened and levelled here and there. The flat on the far side, by the mouth of Valleau Creek (Deer Creek to the locals), was where Theodore Valleau lived, threatened people and attempted to reign supreme by any means, fair or foul. "Foul" could, and occasionally did, mean the use, or threatened use, of the closest weapon within reach, including knife or hand gun, if the stories are to be believed. Those same stories state that Valleau made a regular and visible practice of packin', and tried repeatedly to scare members of the Hamm family into leaving. Such events occurred at the tail end of a small-scale "outlaw" era in the more remote corners of the West Chilcotin.

It was here also that Bert Hamm, and probably one or two of his brothers, built a sturdy house for their parents, Dave and Sarah—after Valleau had vacated the area, I presume. That building is still standing firm but a touch forlorn across a small field. I have seen a photo of that building in its younger years, with a full garden growing and people gathered in front of it enjoying a family celebration. When they finally arrived at Bluff Lake, the Hamm family and Joe Schuk borrowed a small boat and ferried their belongings in trips down the length of the lake. Bert Hamm built the little tumbledown log shack at the north end of the lake, just before the bluffs, to shelter his 1928 Plymouth, which had carried the second Hamm group across the country from Saskatchewan.

As I travel through some of these more remote corners of the West Chilcotin, I have come to realize that this country is significantly different from the eastern plateau closer to the Fraser River. The west is generally higher, wetter, wilder, more marginal and considerably chillier, and the great coastal mountains, fast rivers and high glaciers shape the quality and spirit of life out here. Most dramatically, some of the characters who chose to dwell here, both settler and Indian, lived lives on the edge—or even out past that edge in certain well-known cases. Several were reputed to be on the run. George Powers was one such person, well-liked and respected but said to have been connected to the Plummer Gang in Washington State. George was an early inhabitant of lower Tatlayoko Valley, later selling his place down there to Ken Moore. Legend says he ran off with the lovely Jessie, daughter of a local chief, with her unhappy father and his supporters in pursuit; the true facts are likely much more prosaic. The couple did ranch and trap over in the back of beyond on the east side of Charlotte Lake. George and Jessie lived out their last years at The Gables on the town side of Alexis Creek.

Legend says he ran off with the lovely Jessie, daughter of a local chief, with her unhappy father and his supporters in pursuit.

In more recent times, the semi-legendary Lester Dorsey up at Anahim Lake, about as far west as a fugitive can go before dropping off the Chilcotin Plateau into the Bella Coola Valley, learned many years after the fact that the man down in Washington whose death he thought he was responsible for had carried right on breathing after all.

I believe that West Branch attracted its share of these wild sorts of folks because it was tucked away in the mountains off the main track, a regular "hole in the wall" and little more than a rumour to most people on the outside.

Of course, a few aboriginal people ranged down the valley in the old days, but Lee Butler, of partial First Nations descent himself, is clear that it was Theodore Valleau who drove them out. "Bullshit Belloo," as he was called locally, scared them with his wild and violent, if not crazy, antics and claimed the place as his own. Only a few returned, and many still

81

avoid the valley, Lee states. The conspicuous exceptions in those times were Neganie Guichon and Eagle Lake Henry, both of whom guided survey and mountaineering expeditions down into that big mountain country to the southwest, and even Henry walked around Bullshit Belloo. Other notable exceptions were Lucy (Dagg) Sulin, who died just a few years ago after a long and eventful life, and her mother, Louise One Eye Turner. When Lucy was a child, they would camp and trap down Mosley Creek by Twist Lake with her stepfather, the redoubtable George Turner, a man not easily threatened.

I wonder if that nexus of Valleau-type negativity created some sort of spiritual black hole that spooked people back then. There were wild men, considered dangerous beings who dwelled beyond the limits of regular everyday existence, in the minds of many folks in those times. I wonder if, to some, "bullshit" was an otherworldly spirit reference signifying "illusion," "untrue," "evil"—like the word *mesachie*, which means "bad" or "mean-spirited" in the old Chinook language. Some were a little afraid of Chiwid too, I gather: afraid of what she was, what she might become, what made her that way, what she might stand for, what she might do. Everybody took note when she passed by. Were Theodore Valleau and Lily "Chiwid" Skinner, in some wild way, parallel souls living just a hair over on the other side past the edges of this familiar world? Or, in the case of Monsieur Valleau, were the people of the West Chilcotin simply describing an unpredictable and sometimes dangerous individual? Did the names "Bullshit" and "Belloo" just have a good ring when you pronounced them out loud?

Sage Birchwater lived in this part of the Chilcotin from the late seventies until just a few years ago. He took over Bert Hamm's old trapline and, with his then partner Yarrow (now Christine Peters), lived and trapped martens and squirrels many miles down in the bowels of lower Mosley Creek. They made a minimalist living in that lonely country for nine years, and he has remarked that they were likely the closest inhabitants to Mount Waddington, highest peak by far and a mighty presence in a range of tall peaks in the Coast Mountains. Somewhere during that period of his life, Sage found the inclination and time to talk to and record the memories of a number of the older people in the region. Much of this material became his book *Chiwid,* now a Cariboo–Chilcotin classic; some of the rest he put together into a small collection about, and called, *Valleau.*

The word Sage Birchwater uses to describe Valleau is, charitably, "erratic"; he was amenable one moment, threatening violence and mayhem the next. Sage's main sources on the wild man of West Branch were Randolph Mulvahill of Chezacut, Clayton Mack of *Bella Coola Man* fame, Hank Law, Lee Butler and members of several surveying and mountaineering expeditions who wrote accounts of their travels. Their stories describe the feared Valleau and an amazing array of characters who came into this corner of the country, including the well-known and successful rancher and horse breeder Eagle Lake Henry Sill,

Sage Birchwater and Pogie near the mouth of the Chilcotin River. Photo courtesy of Peter Stein.

who was competent in all aspects of bush and horse lore, and a deadly shot, and who appears to have been afraid of nobody; Neganie Guichon, son-in-law of Old Guichon, who some suggest was shot (a few say by Eagle Lake Henry himself), although Lee Butler is certain he was dragged to death by a horse over at Pinto Lake; Pete McCormick, the ace packer in the country; and Lee's grandmother's husband Jim Holt, who was a big tough cowboy and had a heavy-duty reputation of his own. Clayton Mack, also known to be a pretty fair bullslinger, shared a cabin with Holt one long Chilcotin winter. Mack claimed Holt owned up to a whole list of nefarious deeds, not least of which was horse-stealing south of the border.

Perhaps, in a land of storytellers and bullshit artists, these stories were just more of the same, with the old familiar larger-than-life qualities we have come to associate with backcountry storytelling the world around. Or maybe these guys were just bushed. I've got to think those steep-sloped snow-covered mountains down there closed in on folks in those short dark days of winter, particularly if you lived on the shady side of the valley. Normally, it seems, most of these fellows were pleasant enough to get along with, until somebody brought out the booze. Bill Bliss remarked that Eagle Lake Henry's kids would hide his ammo when the homebrew was ready to tap. But Valleau was potential trouble any time.

Valleau was sure he had sole rights to the entire Mosley Creek valley, all the way down to the Homathko River in the heart of the mountains, and was equally sure he was a fearsome gunslinger, so watch out West Branch. Predictably, then, he was at the centre of nearly all the feuds happening. He was supposed to have shot at Johnny Hamm and Bob Nicholson, husband of Annie, when the two men were in the process of settling farther down Mosley Creek below Valleau's place. Lee Butler says the bullet came very close to Johnny. Lee also says Valleau's cabin was peppered with bullet holes, and the sound of gunshots would occasionally resound from his place. Valleau did put in jail-time for burning down Bob Pyper's store at Chilanko Forks, and claimed he had good reason. Clayton Mack stated he made a living stealing horses and trading them. Certainly he had a running feud with Pete McCormick over stolen horses (with Valleau accused of doing the stealing) and ongoing fights with Jim Holt over who was the biggest hombre in the country, again with Bullshit the likely instigator. His hassles with Holt seemed to unfold as a natural matter of course, like breathing.

Valleau was bound to have problems with Eagle Lake Henry, who had some people in the country, including Katie Schuk, a young girl over at Tatlayoko at that time, at least a little worried. "I was afraid of him," Katie says flatly, commenting on Henry's early reputation. While some were sure he was dangerous, others, like Bill Bliss, who hunted horses with him, said Henry "was a nice guy" except when he was drinking. And June Draney, whose mother, Mary Jane Dagg, was adopted and raised by Henry and Allietta, seemed warm and respectful toward her "Grandpa Henry." Perhaps, like so many of us, Henry mellowed as he aged.

Enter the near-mythical George Turner, a man with a reputation, deserved or otherwise. Turner was thought to have run with and/or from the Dalton Gang down in the United States and came up to the wild West Chilcotin country to get away from it all. The myth includes the famous confrontation Turner, double-bitted axe in hand, had at Engbretson's place at Towdystan with members of the gang, who had, supposedly, followed him up here. According to the stories, the visitors eventually backed down. Turner was believed to be tough but likely wanted no trouble. He had a wife he loved, Louise One Eye, daughter of Chief One Eye. Standard knowledge suggests that the chief was bushwhacked, and a few

Eagle Lake Henry and Allietta Sill. Photo courtesy of Sage Birchwater.

rumours even imply it was Turner who did the shooting, something to do with taking up with the chief's daughter. However, the fact would seem to be that Chief One Eye died of natural causes without help from anyone else. Lee Butler says he lost his eye using black gunpowder to start a fire back in the not-all-that-old trade musket days; he threw too much powder on the fire and it blew up in his face.

George just seems to have wanted to get on with his life. That wasn't enough to stop him from getting into a scrap with Valleau, however. George and Louise were trapping down the West Branch, and Bullshit tried to drive them out. Based on the stories, it's not hard to imagine Valleau, a powder keg and feeling he had something to prove, attempting to incite a fight. Turner claimed "Valloo" left strychnine-laced salmon in his cabin. He tasted it and spat it out. Lee says Turner got out of the area for fear he'd lose control and kill Valleau. According to Lee, some policeman told George, "Why don't you shoot him yourself, if you see him?" "Yeah right, you'd just love that," George is said to have replied.

When Valleau took that shot at, or by, Johnny Hamm, they say you could hear the bullet ripping through the willows. But with that incident, Butler maintains Valleau scared himself enough to get out of the country and move on up to Burns Lake a year later, taking his goats with him, I presume. (He had stomach trouble, apparently, and needed the milk.) I am curious as to whether he escaped out the back route, north past Anahim and Ulkatcho lakes and Anahim Peak, major source of obsidian in the region since time's beginning. There was an old network of trails across the Ootsa Lake country before Kenney Dam was built, flooding out the vast Nechako River system to power the aluminum smelter at Kitimat.

The fact is, people did get killed in this land in those old days. Individuals did disappear out there on the fringes. Some of those men lived by different rules if they lived by rules at all. Euro-culture at large, with its boundaries and its built-in checks and balances, was just beginning to touch the far western reaches of this country. Aboriginal folks were still decimated, in shock from disease, deaths and culture change, and for the most part, except for a few alpha individuals like Eagle Lake Henry, just surviving. "Lawn'order" was stretched thin.

Clayton Mack, a "marvellous storyteller," according to Cliff Kopas, but who, nonetheless, must be read with a large pinch of salt, refers in a section of *Bella Coola Man* to an incident that took place in the remote northern lake country. A certain individual shot an inhospitable settler for his lack of charity and good manners, then shot the man's partner as the latter came down the trail a few minutes later. Who was there to stop him? Who was there to prove it? We know this story is likely true because the shooter's brother, a well-known man who had a cabin out on the grease trail, claimed he was present and witnessed it all. I spotted a picture of the perpetrator and recognized his name in a book of Harlan Smith's Bella Coola Valley field photos. The man looked soul-racked and haunted. In the next photo, his sharp-featured wife appeared hard-eyed and unwell, as if she knew the truth and had to live with it.

Over the years, these old tales and rumours accrue a hazy authority with time and telling, and take on the qualities of myth; myth tales have their own ways of reverberating and deepening as they echo around the mountains. Hints of old attitudes, values and ways of seeing and hearing persist today in corners of the Chilcotin backcountry.

The members of the Hamm family, Johnny, Bert, Annie Nicholson, various spouses and children, and Joe Schuk, came to the area in two waves in about 1932 and 1936. As Johnny could have attested, Valleau was still around; in fact, it was Valleau himself, in a rare moment of unguarded generosity, who invited members of the first wave down to his valley, enticing them with stories of the good vegetables he grew there. These intrepid emigrants from dried-out Saskatchewan encountered many difficulties on their way west to establish their new lives in that new and strange Chilcotin land. Joe Schuk says that in 1936, when he and the Hamms followed the wagon trail into the West Branch, he had to get out and scout ahead on foot to spot signs of the route. Johnny Hamm had already arrived and homesteaded down-valley past Valleau Creek. Annie and Bob Nicholson settled a half mile farther on. Making a living was tough, money-making opportunities were scarce and, over time, some of the group vacated—most notably Bob, who left Annie behind to look after their five children, Ora, Don, Lorna, Ula and Terry.

The heart of Annie's story is that she carried on. In her characteristically indomitable manner, and with her loving, motherly courage, she became something of a local legend. In contrast to some of the earlier, wilder inhabitants of West Branch, Annie Nicholson, and others like her, demonstrates the power and value of caring, duty and civility in ways not so evident before. Her old home still stands down the valley, with its complex of mostly little outbuildings around it, and a single clump of rhubarb resolutely growing in the rich loam above Mosley Creek where her famous vegetable garden used to be.

I first saw the Nicholson place in the early eighties, when Don Brooks and I drove by on a preliminary excursion into the southwest Chilcotin. I got a better look around the place a year or two later when I took my aged parents, Alizon and Pat, down there on one of our annual trips into some of the nooks and crannies of that western country. Our home base was Iris Moore and Dennis Redford's place over at Tatlayoko Lake.

Mum and Dad, who had their own dip into the world of homesteading and guide-outfitting up the North Thompson in the aftermath of the war, loved to prowl around old homesteads and visualize the lives of the ones who had lived there. I can still hear them talking and reminiscing quietly as they walked together. They had no difficulty comprehending the details of those pioneer lives, remembering so sharply the struggles, lack of money, isolation and pleasures of their own years in the bush. I remember those years too, but for me, a child, those times were just life. Every day was an adventure. Macaroni, moose and deer meat, fish, porridge and home-canned vegetables seemed fine to me. We were poor, but, as it turns out, our lives were rich. In their own hindsight, those were highlight years for Mum and Dad.

Annie Nicholson's long-vacated home in lower West Branch. Photo courtesy of Tom Hueston.

Judging by the cow shit we found, the old Nicholson house had become a haven for cattle wanting to escape rough weather ... until the floorboards by the door in the main room started caving in, making the place dangerous for bovines and people. Because the house was simply a series of rooms built in sections, end to end, with logs of short lengths so that small arms and backs could lift them, and because the lean-to bedrooms, added one by one as the children grew, were mostly too small for cows, many of the details of the Nicholson family life remained. The extra rooms were each carefully walled with split poplar strips for privacy; dresses still hung in a tiny closet. Doors were hanging off hinges;

window panes were broken; thin, sunbleached cotton curtains flapped; jars, Mason lids, dishware bits, kettles, a bruised blue-enamel basin, and decayed leather shoes and worn gumboots, mainly unmatched, lay about. Notebooks from school, scratched with the blue-ink scrawling of children learning to write and doing their lessons; bills and invoices; scraps of letters from friends and government officials were strewn here and there. Outside, broken tools, worn wooden feeding troughs, stove parts, car parts, farm machinery parts, motor bits, fence pickets, boards with nails, wire, galvanized metal, buckets with holes, tin cans, pipe—most everything rusted—lay in scattered profusion.

Outbuildings abounded, some seeming more recent, some made from lumber, some small, as if built for just a few chickens, maybe a piglet or two, a new puppy, animal by animal, need by need. At least one such construction, made from good lumber, was car related based on the clues: patches of dumped crankcase oil, caked and black; punctured oil cans; shiny nickel-plated bumpers; numerous skinny, treadless, car tires you could just about see through; a collection of licence plates and another of cylinder heads.

Poor folk don't throw stuff away. Those parts and bits "might come in handy sometime," and it was too far to go for replacements, even if there was the cash to pay. Someone could probably fix the current breakdown, one of the kids maybe, or Bern Mullens down the road might invent some new gizmo or thingamabob to get the outfit through for another season. "If we can just haywire the old girl together for one more trip to town, we'll make 'er before winter sets in." I would expect they pulled and straightened used nails and spikes, like most country people back then, conditioned by the dirty thirties. Any useful stuff left around loose would have been long liberated.

Some years after my first visits down there, while in the process with my brothers of dealing with the details of our recently deceased parents' estate, I came upon a thin file folder labelled "West Branch." The few interesting written artifacts it held included several invoices from fur auction sales in the winter of 1953 (Annie trapped mainly martens and squirrels, though she did catch one silver fox that year), one or two business letters and scraps of personal notes, all gathered at Annie's old place by our scavenger mother, Alizon, herself a lifelong saver, and ferreted away for future viewing, cherished reminders of a part of her own country life. One artifact of note was an answer from Pete Yells, of the Department of Highways at Alexis Creek, to Annie's letter requesting a snowplough for the road in wintertime. There had been problems of illness and machine breakdown, apparently, and Len Butler, the grader man (Lee's father), was unable to plough around Bluff Lake. Annie's letter drew an official placating response: "Sorry for your isolation, Mrs. Nicholson." This small, detailed, meaningful slice of a pioneer woman's survival is affecting, and the fact that Mum's heart was touched is equally moving to me. She knew too well how Annie's life had been.

Annie, known to her world as "Trapper Annie," made her family's living not only by trapping but also by any other means she could manage, with some assistance from her old friend Bern Mullens, one of the earliest West Branch pioneers. Annie and Bern ran a small herd of cattle together, and she and her children grew a large vegetable garden, selling or trading their surplus produce. I'd be surprised if she didn't grow flowers also, for the pleasure of their beauty. She cooked for a geological survey party over several summer seasons and eventually obtained a Toyota Land Cruiser for getting around and going to town for supplies; my guess is that when the surveyors had completed their work, they made her an offer she couldn't refuse. Sage Birchwater, who worked for her one summer, tells me she used the Cruiser, towing a dump rake behind, for haying. She would reach out the window to pull on a trip rope to dump the hay as necessary. She and Bern even tried mining together, as much for recreation as for profit.

She was famous for always wearing a dress and stockings, no matter what the activity, even when she was out trapping. One issue of *Hoofprints in History* included an article on Annie and Bern that contains a hair-raising tale of the evening Annie spotted a cougar trailing her as she walked the many miles home from her trapline down by Twist Lake. She shot the animal with her squirrel rifle. When she and son Don returned in daylight, they found the tracks of not one but five cougars, probably a family group, circling Annie's footprints. I picture that nighttime scene in my mind: the beam of her flashlight beyond her gunsights reflecting from the animals' eyes, and Annie in her long dress, doing whatever was necessary to ensure the well-being and safety of her family.

> *She was famous for always wearing a dress and stockings, no matter what the activity, even when she was out trapping.*

Sadly, some of Annie's children died too young. Terry, Lee Butler's close friend, drowned in Schilling Lake on a guiding trip in the Klinaklini Valley while still a young man; his brother Don died at age forty-two, the outcome of a weak heart and pneumonia. The girls married and, one way or another, moved away, leaving Mother Annie alone down there on Mosley Creek, her most obvious purpose in life done. Can you imagine the silence in that small house when the last child departed? Sage remarked that Annie cured a prolonged fit of depression by studiously reading stacks of *Reader's Digest* end to end. I suppose all those stories, perspectives and positive outcomes from far away expanded her context; it would be easy to get bushed down in the bottom of the West Branch.

Annie, her dear friend Bern, and Pat Braid, who lived down-valley, where Walt Foster is headquartered now, were referred to affectionately as the "three Musketeers" in their latter years. At Christmas and other festive occasions, the three would walk or drive up to join the Butler family in celebration. Bern and Pat played violins, and Bev Butler, the accordion; it sounds like jolly times were had by all. The trio, along with Billy Woods, also a fiddler, played for dances. Once, the three old folks decided to travel south to see Vancouver together; the consensus is that these three old echoes of a bygone rural and rustic past could not help but draw attention to themselves as they walked around, spotting and noting the signs of massed urbanization down there in the big smoke.

One of the more touching aspects of Annie's story is her long-time friendship with Bern Mullens. Bern lived another mile or so down the road, near where Mosley Creek begins its serious drop down through the mountains. Through all those years, Bern helped Annie out when he could, especially as they got older. They became close, and when they became elderly and infirm, she moved into Bern's big house with him. But they didn't live as man and wife: they lived, each with their own set of dogs, in opposite corners of the house, separated by plywood partitions, until Annie died finally in 1981. Bern passed on just two months after Annie. Clearly, he could not live without her. Any of us with a deep, long-lasting, spousal heart-connection with another (and I am one, I gratefully state) can understand, profoundly, such concurrence. Their hearts and souls had become fused. It is eternally inspiring to note the myriad of ways in which the unifying power of love finds itself and enacts itself.

WILD LIFE IN THE WEST BRANCH: LEE BUTLER

... neither the land
nor the knowledge of the land can be replaced.
A territory is made perfect by knowledge.

The Other Side of Eden
—Hugh Brody

ANOTHER ADMIRABLE CHARACTER who is alive and fairly well down in West Branch right now is Lee Butler. I had seen and recognized Lee on three brief encounters in the years before I actually met him one recent spring. The first time he was crossing the road to the barn as my old parents and I drove by. Lee was wearing his characteristically weather-beaten, old-style cowboy hat, and I recognized him easily from two sets of articles and photos in *Hoofprints in History*. I do not remember names well, but I do remember faces.

The second time I saw him, I was with my partner, Marne. Lee was on the back end of his tractor, close to the road in front of his home place, digging a posthole and looking as if he was enjoying himself. Our eyes met for a moment, and I had the distinct impression he would not have minded if I'd stopped for a chat or to ask him something. By the time that possibility registered, we were well past; my reactions tend to be slow in such matters. Marne said, "Turn back. Go talk with him." But I replied, "I don't want to be a bother." Now, as I look back, I'm sure he would have welcomed an interruption.

Marne has a typically generous view that a traveller should "go in and buy something"; that way you meet people. With a smile that lights up the world, her system is infallible, for her. That's how we recently met Frank Chendi, the Chilcotin's current wandering legend, for example. He was down in Lillooet working for the beekeeping "Honeyman," a character of some considerable repute himself, and naturally Marne stopped to buy a jar of honey. Chendi and Marne got talking at length about cello lessons for his sweetheart. Frank has found true love, so they say, and is not wandering so much these last years. In his younger days he would walk barefoot down through the mountainous South Chilcotin backcountry, all the long and wild way from his home far to the north on Chilko Lake, sleeping under trees and logs as he travelled to visit his sister in the lower reaches of the Yalakom Valley. Check the distance on a topo map sometime. Note the high ridges and passes he walked over. Lee Butler claims that, in his time, Frank Chendi could out-walk a horse, though I hear his arthritis is acting up these days. Frank, who came originally from the United States, was named "Chendi" by the people over in Nemaiah. *Chendi* means "greenstick" or "jackpine" in Tsilhqot'in.

The third encounter occurred not long ago. Lee was on a horse near Horne Lake, pushing some cows along the road with another rider, a tall, rangy, older guy with glasses. I had a hunch it might have been Foster from down the valley. Lee had a smile on his face like the cat that ate the cream, not wide but deep, like he was doing exactly what he was meant to be doing, riding his saddle horse, accomplishing something useful, living the cowboy life for the moment. He told me later that if a bunch of cattle and riders were going by, he'd be sure to saddle up and join them in a minute just for the fun. "Horses," he said with a little smile, "still my favourite form of transportation." Lee continues to place well at the Tatla Lake gymkhanas.

Lee Butler is one of the more impressive individuals I have had the pleasure to meet out there in Chilcotin land. He is a fount of knowledge, precisely and modestly stated. Lee is directly descended from Nancy Swanson, his great-grandmother on his mother's side. This is a fact that flabbergasts me. We are referring to "the" Nancy Swanson here, the young Tsilhqot'in (Chilcotin) woman who was the partner of William Manning

Lee Butler on his prize mare Ayndee (which means "thunder and lightning" in Tsilhqot'in) at the Tatla Lake gymkhana grounds by Martin Lake. Photo courtesy of Lee and Bev Butler.

during the Chilcotin troubles in the spring of 1864. Manning, the first settler at Puntzi Lake, northeast of Tatla Lake, chose to locate his farm on a traditional campsite; in fact, he drove some Tsilhqot'in people off to do so. Several Tsilhqot'in men shot him and later dumped his body in the nearby creek. Nancy had tried to warn him, but he would not listen. She gave testimony in front of Judge Matthew Begbie at the ensuing trials. Lee has copies of the notes from that event. Manning's killing was one of the four or five episodes that comprised the Chilcotin War, the main event of which occurred a few weeks earlier down the Homathko River, where fourteen members of Alfred Waddington's road-building crew were killed, possibly by some of those same people.

Later, Nancy married Bill Swanson, a horse rancher and "spud farmer" on the Fraser River across from the mouth of Chimney Creek. Swanson had come to the area during the Cariboo goldrush. They had two daughters, one of whom, Annie, became wife of Jim MacKill (founder of the lodge at One Eye Lake) and Lee Butler's grandmother.

In the first few pages of Eric Collier's Chilcotin classic *Three against the Wilderness*, Collier depicts an old Indian lady who lived up behind what is now Chilcotin Lodge at Riske Creek. She became known to him as Lala, grandmother of Lillian, the future Mrs. Collier, but her formal (non-aboriginal) name was Nancy Swanson. By the time Collier knew her, she was ancient. She had great understanding of the country, and it was she who told Collier that beavers and their dams were the key to the liveliness of the more northerly forested lands. Her teaching inspired him to reintroduce and assist beavers in restoring the trapped-out country around Meldrum Creek and selectively trap them for a living.

That Nancy Swanson connection makes Lillian Collier something like Lee Butler's second cousin, so Eric Collier is connected to Lee by marriage.

Nancy Swanson's gravesite behind Chilcotin Lodge at Riske Creek. Photo courtesy of John Schreiber.

As I say, up here we find, sooner or later, that most everybody is related, at least distantly, to most everybody else. Nancy is buried in the little cemetery with the white picket fence that gleams so brightly through the trees on the Palmantier property, up past Chilcotin Lodge. Recently, after finding nobody home at Palmantier's, I walked up through the bush behind the lodge to the cemetery to acknowledge her presence up close.

I finally arranged to meet Lee down at West Branch in June 2006. It was the first of half a dozen interesting get-togethers. I arrived at the Butler ranch to find Lee up on his roof, replacing a chimney pipe and fixing some flashing. I joined him up there for a few minutes; except for a little roof talk, we were silent while he finished the job. We did agree that our respective capacities for good balance in high places were not what they used to be. It's funny how we old-timers talk about what we can't do anymore. Lee was an agile seventy-seven.

He had pulled up two chairs in his front yard; I proffered my gift of a little beef jerky from Longview, Alberta—Ian Tyson's home ground—and we settled in to talk. He began by saying he didn't have much to say, but if I asked questions, he'd see if he could answer them. Well, I had lots of questions, a partial list of good detailed ones, to ask, and Lee had a considered answer for nearly all of them. He never overstates. We were to talk of many things, but we began by discussing wildlife.

Lee had obviously studied animals throughout his life, both as a fundamental element of survival and because they are invariably interesting. He proceeded to comment on the general state of game birds these days: ducks are generally more plentiful in the area now, especially widgeons and mallards; brant don't come through here anymore but, as we might expect, Canada geese are more plentiful than ever. Lee thought snow geese were losing ground. I told him of their good winter numbers in the Lower Mainland and assured him that, generally, I thought they were doing well. I had heard their breeding grounds up on Herschel Island in the Arctic were overpopulated to the point of causing serious erosion and suggested they could use some thinning. I commented that a hundred years earlier they were hunted for their feathers. "Like whooping cranes," he said. I nodded.

"I don't see so many pintails now," he remarked. "They're on the critical list, I think."

Ah, those most elegant pintails, among my favourite bird species, I thought, picturing their subtle colouration and lines, their slim grace, their quiet. Some bird species are quiet in their voices, in their movements, in their being. Cedar waxwings are like that; they just sit there, unmoving, where they happen to be perched. So do band-tailed pigeons in their small groups in the tops of tall conifers, if we're fortunate enough to spot them. Their safety would seem to be in numbers.

"You see lots of green-winged teals," Lee said. "You see them with shovellers all the time, but no cinnamons anymore. They used to nest around here. The males go blood-red in the spring."

I told him I hadn't seen that. But more recently I have seen a male cinnamon teal, with the low, late afternoon sunlight hitting his spring plumage just right, shining off him like wet blood. Lee didn't mention the third species in that fast-flying teal family, the blue-winged.

I described the thrill of seeing several thousand spiralling sandhill cranes near Keremeos, catching a thermal above us off the hillside behind Causton and soaring out of sight.

"I've seen that here," said Lee. There was a note of excitement in his voice. "They're gathering cranes together from all over." To head south, I imagined.

I asked my perennial question: "Were there really bighorn sheep down the Homathko River?"

Lee said that, yes, there were California bighorns on the steep, south-facing, open (and probably windblown) slopes above the river between Nude and Ottarasko creeks. He said it looked like they wintered in the Tatlayoko Valley, below Niut Mountain, by what is Les Harris's home place now, where long groves of caterpillar-killed poplars stand. Harris told him there were sheep bones and ram skulls all through there. Theodore Valleau ran sheep and goats not many miles away, and Lee figured the wild ones died of lungworm, caught from contact with the domestics. He said there used to be bighorns across the valley from his place, in the rocks on the west side. We both thought those bands would have been marginal, probably split off from the bighorn bands around Nemaiah.

A silver thaw had killed off the elk in this country back in the early 1800s, but Lee maintained that elk occasionally wandered down here from up north around Quesnel, and I had heard Chilco Choate over at Gaspard Lake suggest something similar. Nancy Swanson spoke of that lethal thaw to Eric Collier. She said animals, wild and domestic, were unable to break through the ice-covered snow to feed and died all over the region. As well, elk prefer open country, graze in herds, like cattle, and had been easy pickings for musket-carrying meat hunters working for the fur companies in early post-contact days. Deer browse and are more covert, typically not herding up so much.

He found a bear and a big sow of his facing each other, squared off in the dark.

Lee still shoots deer for meat. "About half the beef we eat is off the land," he told me.

The Queen's beef, I thought, noting his use of the word "beef" for wild meat.

He said that if there are black bears in his yard, he shoots them, but he had only ever shot one grizzly, and that was by accident. One night he heard a commotion and thought it was a black bear after his pigs in a field. He found a bear and a big sow of his facing each other, squared off in the dark. He shot it, and in the light of the following day, the carcass turned out to be that of a grizzly. "That high at the hump," he said, indicating about five feet off the ground with his arm. "The hide was seven feet long." Lee added that they see more grizzly these days. "Way more, up and down Mosley Creek, so it's not just the same bears moving around." We discussed the possibility of bears from the coastal inlets wandering up into the Interior, especially as the salmon stocks decline down there; in contrast to females, male grizzlies range widely.

The Butler dog, a labrador-like hound, began barking with a particular intensity. Lee stopped instantly and cocked his head to listen, a hint of a smile on his face. "When they bark that way, there's something back in the bush behind the house," he said eventually, as the dog went quiet. "There are three or four grizzlies around here these days; they just pass through." One, Lee said, is "trophy sized" and moves up and down the creek. He pointed over to where Butler Creek ran, audible but not visible, through the cottonwoods a couple of hundred yards away. "I don't bother him; he doesn't bother me."

"How long has he been around?" I asked.

"Oh, about ten years now," Lee said.

"He's comfortable here then," I said.

He nodded and proceeded to tell me about a mother black bear with four cubs that had been hanging around in the field up the road one spring. He noticed that when he looked at her straight on, she got nervous, but when he began looking at her out of the corner of his eyes as he walked by, she relaxed. Lee demonstrated looking sideways. "Same with walking," he said, "you move sideways."

I replied that I had detected similar reactions with birds and bears both.

Lee described riding horseback by a grizzly that was in a thicket just a few feet off the trail as he passed. "I never turned my head and the horse never knew."

We talked about the power of looking and eye contact. I described the size of eyes, especially the irises, on pole carvings in old Haida villages in the southeast Queen Charlottes (Haida Gwaii). The dog resumed barking; Lee turned sideways to listen.

I told him that when I was young, up the coast, we sometimes used bear grease on our caulk boots. Mum and Dad swore it made the best lard for pie pastry. Lee nodded. The meat from an upland, berry-fed bear wasn't so bad either. My old man only ever shot two or three. The first bear I saw in my life, I saw from my father's shoulders. It was a big black shadow moving off the railroad tracks into elderberry brush near

Butler horses and barns by Butler Creek in the West Branch. Photo courtesy of Marne St. Claire.

Dad's vegetable garden at Camp Three (Nitinat Camp) off the west end of Cowichan Lake. I was barely two years old.

I asked if wolves were getting more plentiful now. Again Lee said, "Way more. I lost two yearlings last year, down at the far end of the field by the lake. I don't usually go down there. I saw a wolf track past Graveyard Springs on the old road to Tatla. It was huge." He held up his hand, fingers splayed (except for one missing digit). "That wide!"

Rainbow trout were running; the creeks were high. As we talked, I heard eagles whinnying in the cottonwoods along Butler Creek, and Lee's horses, excited about something, making a similar sound down at the bottom of his field. We, all of us, were enjoying a warm, late spring day. I remember Lee saying that he wouldn't want to be anywhere else. Like Gary Snyder, my zen poet mentor and exemplar, who says that he lives where he lives, in the Sierra Nevada mountains of central California, as if he will be there for a thousand years.

We moved on to some of the old characters of the country. Some of Lee's statements amaze me: his father, Leonard Butler, had packed for Frank Swannell, the truly legendary surveyor and another of this province's unacknowledged heroes (his absence is conspicuous in the *Encyclopedia of BC*), who traipsed through vast areas of northern BC making maps and naming mountains by the hundreds. They were surveying in the portage area between Eutsuk and Whitesail lakes in the Ootsa Lake country, and up along the Mackenzie Grease Trail. Lee said the conditions and bugs were awful. (I recalled walking that trail along the Kohasganko River with Don Brooks one sunny summer afternoon in 1982 on our way to Tommy Walker's cabin southwest of the Tanya Lakes. We were carrying full packs and fast-trotting to keep ahead of the mosquitoes steaming up out of the swampy ground in clouds around us.)

Shorty Grell (aka Dunn), one of Bill Miner's train-robbing accomplices, worked on Swannell's crew at that time, having served his sentence for the Ducks job east of Kamloops; he would have been a much older man by then. The bespectacled George Powers, an early Chilcotin settler, was on that crew as well.

Lee's grandfather Jim MacKill, who married Nancy Swanson's daughter Annie, was a "big, tall Scotsman" and former policeman. Jim and Annie built and ran the big-game hunting lodge at One Eye Lake. Their daughter Hilda was Lee's mother. Lee said he was slightly afraid of his grandfather. Hilda's brother Clarence was a guide himself and later ran the One Eye place. Of his uncle, Lee said, "When there was a job to do, he did it well." The terseness of his comment made me think there might be more to Clarence than he let on. Clarence, Hilda and her husband, Leonard, are buried in a tidy row in the cemetery on the ridge above Tatla Lake, uphill from the Grahams and below Sarah Schuk and the brothers McGhee. My guess is that Jim and Annie MacKill were buried at One Eye Lake.

We talked briefly about Betty (Graham) Linder, who is also up there in a section of the Graham family plot. Betty was known to be kind-hearted and earned a reputation for helping people. "She was kinda like that Jane Bryant [Jane Bryant Lehman, the famous nurse up at Anahim Lake]. Betty gave me my first bath when I come into this country," Lee said with a big smile on his face.

I thought that would have taken place at the big Graham house on the way home from the little Red Cross hospital at Alexis Creek; the roads were slow going three-quarters of a century ago. Lee began his "coming into this country" at the moment of conception.

I asked about Baptiste Dester, also a guide and a competent log-house man, who sometimes worked for the MacKills. "Another good old guy," said Lee. George Turner, the presumed outlaw, was also "a nice old guy." Lee said that Valleau, aka Bullshit Belloo, "thought he was tough; Charlie Parks and he had a fight. Parks was bigger, but he lost." According to Lee, Jim Brown, the old trapper and prospector who lived west of Chignell's Halfway Ranch, talked in a "high-pitched squeal."

Thomas Squinas, son of old Chief Domas Squinas, was "short and thickset" and a "real good man." Lee met him at Lester Dorsey's funeral in the 1970s. Thomas's wife, Celistine, had become friends with Lee's mother, and Celistine and her family used to pick berries where Butler's field is now. Lee's dad, Leonard, knew Maxie Heckman, the one-armed trapper and ex-miner who gave his name to the pass into the Bella Coola Valley. Clayton Mack claims Heckman was the true father of famous packer Josephine Robson and of Clayton's wife, Doll—not, as most people believed, Anton Capoose, the shrewd old trader and packer of his day. Josephine, who died in the early 1990s at Saddle Horse Meadow east of Heckman Pass, was a hunter, a deadly shot and a fine judge of moosemeat on the hoof. She is also Marne's heroine, and Marne and I went especially to see her grave at Capoose Crossing on the Dean River below Anahim Lake. It was situated close to a deadfall wolf trap, with a dried-out wolf carcass looking nondescript and smaller-than-life in the dust beside it.

Josephine was a hunter, a deadly shot and a fine judge of moosemeat on the hoof.

I learned that Chief One Eye and his son-in-law George Turner were buried along the shore of One Eye Lake past the Forestry campsite to the east, on a little point. Apparently George had requested to be buried next to the old chief, father of his beloved Louise. I meant to ask where she had found her final resting ground. Their daughter Mary Ann Ross, reputed to have been gorgeous, was alive in Williams Lake until recently. Lee mentioned that Cal Wycott, son of Stranger Wycott down at Churn Creek, died at Moon's ranch in the late thirties. Pete McCormick, packer and guide to some of the mountaineering and surveying expeditions in that West Chilcotin country, died in the forties and was buried up the hillside from his place at Clearwater Lake. Marne and I did a quick search across that sidehill for his gravesite when we were passing through one time, but missed it. In the brush, a wooden head board would rot quickly.

Lee had been a guide-outfitter himself for a while and, feeling slightly overwhelmed by the volume of personal detail so far—all of it fascinating—I asked him how he had liked guiding. He said he had guided lots of hunters. In the early years, most of them didn't care if they got game or not; they were just out there for the enjoyment and usually got game anyhow. As time went on, though, the business became more difficult, especially as clients, mainly from the United States, demanded he guarantee they'd bag their limit, as if that was possible. One party from Kansas told him they would "have to deal elsewhere if Lee could not guarantee them a full limit"—which in their particular case was one black bear and two moose. It was then that Lee decided he'd had his fill of guiding and quit.

Like all the small ranchers in the Chilcotin trying to scrape out a living, Lee had worked at a wide variety of jobs to bring in cash. He trapped, drove school bus, ran bulldozer and worked for the Ministry of Highways, getting to be a good mechanic in the process. He expressed a modest pride in his ability to monkey-wrench his diesel tractor. He worked on a survey for BC Hydro, assessing possible dam sites down the Homathko River. In that job he got the opportunity to ride down lower Mosley Creek in a river boat, and while working near the Waddington Road

Pete McCormick, old-time horse packer from Clearwater Lake in the West Chilcotin. Photo courtesy of Bev Butler.

massacre site, he found an antique fork hidden in a hole in a tree, most likely put there for safekeeping by some nameless pilferer from that original time. Lee said he had circled in a helicopter over Fury Gap and Franklin Glacier, as well as the great mountain bearing the name of the Victoria merchant Alfred Waddington, mastermind of that dubious and ill-fated road-building venture up through the Homathko canyon into the Interior. He was in awe of the sheer expanse of ice, square miles of it, with myriad hidden, snow-covered crevasses, and the massive knife-edged peak itself. Lee said, slightly incredulous, "If you happened to land on a glacier up there and couldn't get off again, you'd die" because of the cold and the vast rawness and isolation of the country.

He was in awe of the sheer expanse of ice, square miles of it, with myriad hidden, snow-covered crevasses, and the massive knife-edged peak itself.

I was compelled to ask Lee for his take on Donald McLean, the former Hudson's Bay Company man who had been in charge at Fort Chilcotin, and later at Klus-kus up on the grease trail, and who was hated by most Indian people who knew him—likely for good reasons, if we are to believe the stories. "A hit man for the Hudson's Bay," Lee replied with a touch of vehemence. He firmly repeated himself on that point at another of our meetings.

McLean, father of the wild McLean boys, had a reputation for cruelty. As one of the leaders of the Cox expedition, on the trail of the perpetrators of the Waddington Road killings, he knew he was marked and wore metal body armour under his coat. The shooters set up a low decoy to induce him to bend over and expose his chest enough so they could shoot him. That event, the final episode of the Chilcotin War, is supposed to have taken place close to the west end of Big Eagle Lake, near a little creek, in the vicinity of Patrick Charleyboy's place. "He had it coming," said Lee. I asked where, along the south shore of the lake, the shooting had taken place, and he explained that a drift fence, to keep cattle from escaping down the lake, now marked the location of McLean's last moments on this Earth.

The hours of our first meeting rolled by quickly. Lee Butler is modest, but he has the quiet authority of a man with sure knowledge of who he is and where he lives. He considers questions carefully, and his comments are anchored by the specifics of time, season, place and distance. He is one of those competent woodsmen who asks questions and takes the time to find good answers. My friend Tom Hueston is like that, as was my father, Pat. Lee's discussion of the area, its animals, people and events of the last hundred years was underlain by his unassuming treatment of it all. There are two types of storytellers, I've noticed: those who overstate and those who understate. Both styles have their pluses. My experience is that understated storytellers speak with greater authority; they appear to have less to prove, and they draw us into their story.

At one point, shaking my head with feeling, I exclaimed, "Lee, you sure know a lot."

He looked up at me, his glance quick, and in a small voice asked, "Do you really think so?"

"Oh yeah," I said, trying not to overstate myself.

One of Lee and Bev's young adopted children came out from the house, excited about a plant she had transplanted. She called him "Granddad." Lee responded respectfully in a low voice, and they examined it for a minute or two. Bev came out with cups of coffee for us. The Butler horses, about a dozen of them, had gathered at the fence across the road, looking warm and happy, tails switching, sunlight reflecting off their broad rumps.

Lee and Bev Butler and their young family: Chris, Kathy and Lea (in the back). Photo courtesy of Marne St. Claire.

It was not hard to see that Lee is a sensitive person: his lifetime as a man of the woods has underscored that quality. As we talked, I was aware of his checking, with little looks and pauses, to insure I was still with him. He spoke from within himself, without artifice or pretension; his replies and comments were his best possible truth. He is subtle. A couple of photos from Lee's childhood accompanied articles in the *Hoofprints* series, and I'd say from the pictures of his young face that he was born that way.

In his earlier years he ran afoul of the demon booze. As part of their process of recovery, he and Bev became staunch believers together, active in their church, in their community and in the maintenance of a new life free of alcohol. I would guess that Lee's sensitivity and vulnerability may have helped precipitate his drinking problems. The Butlers are strong believers in the power of prayer; Lee is sure their prayer group is responsible for the cancer falling off his leg, ending his need for chemo. Veera Bonner at Fletcher Lake informed me, subsequently, that Lee told her that prayer had cured another chronic physical affliction that had long given him pain in one of his legs.

There was a question I was dying to ask him, and in one of our meetings I found a way to fit it in. It involved his former brother-in-law, Glen Openshaw, who was once married to his sister Eleanor, now Elora Alden. I'd worked with a Glen Openshaw in the woods at Port McNeill in the early sixties, and I wondered if Lee's Glen was the same guy. Had he, by any chance, worked in the logging industry down on Vancouver Island? Was he a tough, taciturn guy and an extremely hard worker? Did he come originally from the Peace River country? Did he happen to have little or no sense of humour? Was he a hothead, often moody, even sullen? Did he throw stuff?

Turns out he was the same Glen Openshaw all right. We used to call him Glen Openshirt because he walked around with his shirt open to his waist, no matter the weather. He showed up in camp driving a pink Lincoln, about as long as a bunkhouse. We could all see that he fancied himself a cowboy.

On the job, the man ran all day long. So did I, to keep up with him, all the while packing heavy log-loading tongs and dragging kinked and jaggered mainline off the trackloader. You had to trot to get the mainline drum rolling for slack. Glen was hooker-head loader, the boss; I was his second loader. We yarded and loaded logs eight to ten hours a day, five or six days a week.

Yup, that was the guy Lee knew, open shirt, muscles, blond sideburns and all. Apparently, like so many, he developed a drinking problem over time and joined the Seventh Day Adventists in an attempt to fix it. Finally he quit his life as a Chilcotin rancher and left the country and his wife, Eleanor. Lee told a short story about Glen's temper, careful to let the details of the man speak for themselves. I had the sneaking feeling that Lee, although he was impassive on the topic, was not impressed with his now long-gone ex-relative. It's a tiny little world.

In one moment during our second meeting, Lee looked me in the face briefly and declared, "I'm First Nations myself." That would be his Nancy Swanson heritage; there was aboriginal blood on his father's side also. It occurred to me as he spoke that he looked more Indian in his old age than in those pictures from his youth. I asked him how coming into the aboriginal part of his culture had become meaningful to him. He explained that he and Bev go to the gatherings at Tsuniah, Henry's Crossing, Siwash Bridge and up at Red Brush. They meet relatives, including relatives they didn't even know they had, and listen to the old people. "Some of them spend time with you and read you like a book," he said. One old lady, Adele Billy, a strong Christian, is teaching him and Bev how to fish in the old-time ways.

I remembered Red Brush, off on its own in a morass of hay meadows and moose swamps up in that big wide spruce and pine country towards the Itcha Mountains northwest of Puntzi Lake. That's woodland caribou territory. I went there on a shiny, nippy weekend in October of 1970 with John Rathjen, who drowned in Alkali Lake trying to save a life not many years later. We came around the corner of the tiny church and startled the heck out of a young woman in a bright headscarf and long skirt, who was bent over shoeing her saddle horse. We quickly apologized for the scare. She was all by herself but for her rosy-faced, bundled-up button of a daughter, sitting on the steps of the little church, watching.

I asked Lee how you find the place now that the Satah Mountain logging road runs through there. "There's a wagon track off the main road to the right. You drop down. It's a short distance," he answered, "but somebody's got to pretty well show you. We went up for New Year's Day there once. We built a fire by the old church and celebrated."

"Were you ever interested in Indian spirituality?" I asked.

"Yeah, they talk about the Creator. We figure it's the same thing, just a different angle. We think they go off on some things."

I asked, "Like what?"

"Like the mountain talking to you."

I told Lee about my times up and around and with Ts'yl-os, the great mountainous eminence, over ten thousand feet tall, overlooking Nemaiah Valley. I told him Don Brooks and I had climbed it and gotten sick and weak halfway up. Don dry-heaved for half a day. I figured

I'd come to feel everything about Ts'yl-os was alive.

we'd been rude or careless or stared or pointed at it. I said that I'd come to feel everything about Ts'yl-os was alive, just as Eniyud (Niut Mountain) and her stony kids looking out over Tatlayoko Lake were alive too.

"Definitely," he said. "If I'd climbed up it, I'd expect something." Lee went on to tell the story of Rayfield Alphonse and a friend of his, "a couple of young bucks who didn't give a shit for anything," who at the time cowboyed for Chilco Ranch. They were out working off the Nemaiah road somewhere in late summer, probably looking for cows, and a cold snap hit. "Thirty below," Lee said, "dressed for summer. They nearly died. Folks at the Chilco got worried about them and sent out warm clothes and food."

On my third visit with Lee he showed me his picture of Annie MacKill, his grandmother, daughter of the legendary Nancy. It was a grey old photo, a fine picture, fairly large, framed and under glass, but it was easy to see that Annie was a handsome, smiling woman; she looked tall and strong and held herself with dignity. Lee held her image up with pride. I would like to have gotten a photo of the expression on his face and on Annie's in the picture.

We talked of some of the kekuli pithouse sites in this country, mentioning a few specific locations: the south end of Little Sapeye Lake, Lava Canyon on the Chilko River, and another on the Chilko upstream from Henry's Crossing. "There are twelve pits there, and crosses, about five, including one big one."

"Why there, and when?" I asked.

"There's steelhead there in winter, under the ice," Lee replied. He was pretty sure the priests put the crosses there in the 1840s.

I asked him why, though we did find a stone-lined storage pit on a gravel esker, there seemed to be no kekuli pit sites at what looked like an obvious location at the north end of Tatlayoko Lake.

"That was a sacred hunting area," he answered.

Why sacred? I asked myself (sometimes I find the S-word a mite overused). Then it occurred to me that sites with the right conditions for wintering bighorn sheep are scarce, especially in marginal territory like Tatlayoko, close in to the big, deep-snow Coast Mountains. Aboriginal folks, back in those tough old hungry days of subtle subsistence, would have understood that even a semi-permanent human settlement close by would scare a valuable meat source away, perhaps cause it to die off, just as wildlife retreats, dies and disappears now when we move, in our multitude of ways (jet boats, ATVs, heli-skiing, open-pit mining or simply nature loving), into their territories.

I said, "I've got a question for you, Lee, that I probably know the answer for already, but I'll ask you anyhow: what keeps you going? What gets you through?"

He answered almost before I finished. "The Lord! Without Him, my life would be a complete mess." He spoke with a near explosive certainty,

Niut Mountain (Eniyud) and offspring above Tatlayoko Lake. Photo courtesy of Marne St. Claire.

as if the memories of some experiences were tough to live with.

I understood and told him, "I'm interested in spiritual matters myself." I was referring to subtle ways of living, seeing, being and surrendering.

"Yeah," Lee answered, "I figured you were."

I had almost forgotten to give him a small offering of a box of Scottish shortbread I had brought. Lee gave me a twinkly smile as I passed it to him. His dog began barking in that certain way, and I left Lee standing there in his yard with that little smile of his, head cocked, listening.

Souls, our most subtle aspect, weighted faintly by the substance of the Earth, must link to place a little, no matter how slight the tendrils.

On the cemetery ridge overlooking the community of Tatla Lake and the mountains above West Branch beyond, the people—Len and Hilda Butler, Clarence MacKill, Baptiste Dester, Betty Linder, Bob Graham, Sarah Schuk, the McGhees, and all the others—are laid out, memorialized, remembered, resting, waiting, doing whatever it is that souls in such a place do, or do not do. Resonances of Chiwid pervade, at least for some of us. Souls, our most subtle aspect, weighted faintly by the substance of the Earth, must link to place a little, no matter how slight the tendrils. Small creatures rustle in the grasses. Poplar leaves flutter. Hawks circle. Spirit is light.

A day later, in the sunshine on the north end of the Potato Mountain ridge not far from the top, above Tatlayoko Lake, I pause from walking. With as much attention and deference as I can muster, and feeling the power of this high, stony, deep world, I stand and acknowledge the rocky ridge in front of me to the south, and jagged Niut Mountain (Eniyud) across the lake to the west. I am moved to face each of the four cardinal directions slowly, carefully—east, south, west and north—and the two vertical, up to the sky and down through the earth, as walkers and riders on this continent, out alone on the country, have done since time's beginning. This is a way to acknowledge where we are and, perhaps, who and what we are. Ts'yl-os, Eniyud's former partner, sits far to the southeast past Chilko Lake, a great, white, pointed and, it is said, ill-tempered presence looking out over Nemaiah. I nod cautiously in its/his direction. With new twist ties, I attach little offerings of tobacco to alpine fir branches near at hand, one for each mountain.

When I look out across at the steep stone massif that is moody Eniyud, with her sharp-edged offspring to one side of her, it is almost as if we look face to face, as equals. The space between us is clear, pure emptiness. But except perhaps in some quintessential way, we are not equal at all; the mountain has been here so many eons longer than I, absorbed so much more of the region's unfolding. Time would not seem to be an issue for her, although she too does wear down—just much, much more slowly. For me right now, time slows. In such an extended moment, in such a place, a sense of unity, of completion, however fleeting, is as close as a glance, a slight shift and narrowing of the eyes, a small, almost indiscernible, movement of the hand, a brief pause and surrender, a letting go to vastness: a connection to all that is.

Behind, in the far blue distance, a mass of tall, snowy mountain peaks, glaciers, ridges, rock faces and deep, hidden valleys stretch southeast and northwest along the great, long spine of the Coast Range all the way to and into Alaska. These mountains are lively. "The blue mountains are constantly walking," Dōgen states. In the world of myth, they are living beings.

Across the lake west and south of Eniyud, mountains shine white in the late spring light: Razorback, Blackhorn, Whitesaddle in the back;

Ottarasko farther south; Success, Reliance, Determination, Mantle and Queen Bess beyond all of that. Behind the sheer stone being that is Eni-yud is the valley of the West Branch. At the upper end of that valley, the people, living and deceased, inevitably, by their very existence, give to the presence of the place.

THE CONSTANT ELEGANCE OF TERNS

A north wind, always that travelling
Wind, drums the door.
The reader is listening.
A wolf pauses at the meadow's edge
and quickly enters your heart.

"Quixote in the Snow"
—Charles Lillard

I ONLY EVER saw Donald Ekks one time. It was at the Redstone Rodeo in the summer of 1999. I had not met or seen his wife, Emily, in person, and now, after a lengthy and, from what I understand, fruitful life, she has crossed over the great divide.

My brother Chris and I, with Don Brooks, Dana Devine and friends, were returning from a semi-aborted canoe trip to the Turner Lake chain, above the Atnarko River, at the head of the Bella Coola Valley west of the Chilcotin Plateau. Our goal had been to canoe to Kidney Lake at the upper end of the Turner chain, then climb the ridge southwest of there for a look across at the Monarch and Talchako ice fields in the core of the Coast Range. This is some of the most seriously remote mountain and glacier country in British Columbia. But we were rained, fogged and just about flooded out by a socked-in, extended West Coast deluge without cease. I knew that the all-too-familiar, heavy-branched cedar and mountain hemlock we were brushing through on the portage to our second campsite at Widgeon Lake was too wet-coasty to be anything but a bad sign. I do most of my backcountry rambling in the dry Interior for good reason. As well, Chris and I had developed back ailments—he, a muscle strain; me, back spasms—as a consequence of hoisting my cow of a fibreglass canoe over several portages with the usual excessive Schreiber vigour. So we were both a little relieved that we chose to cut the trip short and leave.

Our waterlogged enterprise did have its moments of epiphany however: a silent, late-evening paddle and drift with my brother on a mirror-like lagoon behind our first camp at the top end of Turner Lake; and, on our last morning out, the quick, bright sight of seven or eight terns passing close by. We had just decided to cut our losses, turn the trip around and make our way back down the lake chain. Glancing up from stuffing damp gear into my canoe bag, I was struck instantly by the birds' angular grace in flight. At that same moment, I realized the little flock was flying not with but into the face of a blustering southwesterly wind coming at us from up the lake. In one of those deep gut-comprehensions we experience occasionally, I knew that in order to carry out their unimaginably long and difficult journey south, these terns must feel out air seams, back eddies and still places, those spaces with least resistance, and, twisting and turning, fly between and around and under the bursts of wind blowing at them. The season is short; the birds must maintain their southward flight; there is no time for waiting.

These were arctic terns I believe, not common terns as I had first thought; that bright, light moment was too brief for field marks. They were flying, in their seemingly effortless, elegant, tern way, up Widgeon

Lake on their course along the western edges of two continents all the way to the South Pacific Ocean, past the farthest reaches of South America. There, at the bottom of the world, they would feed and regain their strength for the return flight north. When the mating and nesting urges stirred once more, they would shift directions and fly that same great, not always pacific ocean all over again, end to end, hemisphere to hemisphere, on what most observers consider to be the longest migration on Earth. These terns would fly with certainty and absolute perseverance no matter which way or how hard the wind was blowing; their instincts, their drive and the vast distances allow them no choice.

> *The waters, still rain-swollen and mud-brown, plunged out of sight, more than eight hundred feet straight down into the mists.*

At the end of that same day, after a fast downstream paddle with both current and wind pushing us, we set up our last camp at the lower end of Turner Lake. Later we walked in to the great cirque at Hunlen Falls for a long, deep look. The sky had begun to clear, but the waters, still rain-swollen and mud-brown, plunged out of sight, more than eight hundred feet straight down into the mists roiling up out of that great wide hole in the ground below us. At the footbridge over Hunlen Creek on the way there, Chris got into a spirited vocal exchange with a rarely seen hawk owl, who was objecting to our presence there.

Two days after that, out on the Chilcotin Plateau and away from the still-cloud-covered mountains, the weather had turned mercifully warm and we were basking in it, back troubles, disappointment and all. Chris and I had the Pathfinder pointed east for home, and as we passed the open flats at Redstone Reserve, dust was rising already and cars, pickups, stock trailers, horses, riders and onlookers were gathering at the rodeo grounds across the field below the highway. We decided to stop in to watch the goings-on.

It was a dry rodeo, well run and welcoming, a pleasant place. There was a full program of events: bull and bronc riding, calf roping, steer wrestling, wild cow milking, barrel races, children's events, gossip, laughter, good times. Contestants seemed not to be suffering the range of injuries that normally come from being flung violently and repeatedly from the backs of large animals. There was horseshit, heat and dry dirt, the smell of hotdogs and warm leather, and little kids bouncing up and down on big saddles and big horses everywhere. Behind all was the protracted bawling of perturbed and unhappy cattle, the standard background chorus of bovine discontent with the current order of things.

We bought tickets and found a place to lean back and watch. Riders were gathering at the top of the steep hill behind the rodeo grounds for the mountain race. Their horses were nervous and difficult to manage; the run would be fast, dangerous and straight downhill. This was a wildly different world to our just-concluded immersion back in the high country.

To one side of where we were sitting, an elderly, grey-headed Indian man wearing a checkered western shirt was perched on top of a log picnic table, examining the facets of a piece of brightly coloured, metallic, chocolate bar wrapper as if he was half-mesmerized by it, and viewing the events. He was a spare man, not heavily built, but he looked as if he had led a physical life and I recognized him right off as Donald Ekks. I had seen a picture of him in Sage Birchwater's book on Chiwid, and another of him with Emily and members of the Lulua family, camped out down in that faraway valley between Chilko Lake and the Taseko River on the shadow side of Ts'yl-os Mountain, in Terry Glavin's book about the Nemaiah people and their land claims. As well, I had read references to Donald and Emily in volumes of *Hoofprints in History*. And I'd heard details about them both from Sage and from Bev and Lee Butler. There seemed to me a wistful quality about Donald when I saw him at the rodeo, as if now he was just passing time here in this place.

Donald Ekks lived and worked around the area all his life. His father, Charlie Ekks, had been well known throughout the western country and is mentioned working for Pete McCormick, the packer from Clearwater Lake, in some older accounts of survey expeditions into the Coast Mountains. When Donald was young, he lived and worked with his father around Red Brush in the bush northwest of Puntzi Lake. Donald and his wife, Emily Lulua Ekks (a younger sister of Tommy Lulua, now deceased), were among the last of the aboriginal people still living in something like the old-time ways: they followed the seasonal rounds across the country between Towdystan, Clearwater Lake, West Branch, Tatlayoko and Chilko lakes, and Redstone, ranching, haying and fencing, hunting and berry picking. Much of each year in their later life, the couple lived in a cabin by Cochin Lake, off the road to Tatlayoko south of Tatla Lake. Cochin Lake is rich in sucker fish, a reliable food resource.

Sage has mentioned that Donald showed him a partially intact kekuli pithouse north of Tommy Lulua's old place, by a small lake off the back road down the Chilko River. Donald's brother-in-law Felix Lulua built it years ago for his grandfather Bapstick. That underground house was unusual in that it was square; virtually all other pithouses in the BC Interior were round. Donald told Sage that in his younger years he had lived in a "kiggley hole" himself from time to time. I noticed an ancient, round kekuli hole, nearly filled in, just across the driveway from a stripped-down, thoroughly rusted-out, old-model car body by Tommy's cabin. Such signs

Donald and Emily's cabin at Cochin Lake. Photo courtesy of John Schreiber.

of primordial human occupation, invariably close to water, occur all across the Chilcotin country.

In a *Hoofprints* article, Bev Butler described her years as the hard-working wife of Lee Butler down in West Branch. She mentioned that they would hire Donald Ekks from time to time to help with the many jobs that make up life on a small, backcountry, Chilcotin ranch. She said, "I really enjoyed Donald's company. He would come and visit and tell stories. He was always good to our kids and took them [to be with him where he worked] when I was busy." He would cook them lunch, which included "parts of the deer we never ate, like the guts and stuff. It didn't bother me. They were well fed and happy, and they loved going with Donald."

When my old friend and hiking partner Don—who with his wife, Dana, had organized our abbreviated canoe expedition—and his then young family were camped on the spit down at the head of Tatlayoko Lake one August in the early eighties, he met an old-timer checking out the nearby Homathko River for fish. Don told me that the man was friendly, knowledgeable and interesting to talk with, and I deduced that he must have been chatting with Donald Ekks.

In photos, Donald's wife, Emily, otherwise known as ?Inkel, seems always to be wearing a colourful kerchief around her head, presumably a holdover from old Roman Catholic influences. My memories of my own family's half year at Creekside—now Mount Currie—in the Pemberton Valley in 1950 included strong recollections of older Lillooet (St'at'imc) women in print dresses and aprons, bright kerchiefs and big smiles, sitting on a logjam on the Birkenhead River, snagging salmon. The river was red with sockeye, and the cottonwoods along the banks were a complementary bright golden, all the more magnificent on still-warm, blue-sky autumn days.

In the several photos of Emily that I have seen, even the family picture of her holding her small great-granddaughter in a sunbonnet at an Anahim Lake stampede, Emily maintains, without exception, the same staunchly impassive expression and firmly turned-down mouth. Another picture of Emily, in an article by her granddaughter Brandy Lulua in *Hoofprints*, shows her in a small boat on Cochin Lake, wearing her kerchief and hauling in a fishnet with a clear resoluteness and authority. Sage Birchwater has suggested that it was more than Emily's demeanour and manner that commanded people's attention and respect; as well, "she was as wise as her days were long."

By all accounts she seems to have been a happy person. Bev Butler described how, despite their difficulties with each other's language, they had good times talking with each other and "enjoyed themselves thoroughly while they had tea and laughed." Brandy Lulua spoke admiringly of her grandmother raising eight children and living off the land. Like many First Nations backcountry women of her generation, Emily tanned hides and did leatherwork all her life. Even in her old age she owned a few horses and cows. Brandy described her "ʔetsu" as "a happy, peaceful, knowledgeable and cultured Tsilhqot'in elder" who enjoyed attending rodeos and gatherings.

I was pleased to recognize Doris and Madeline Lulua in attendance at the Redstone Rodeo also. We had passed their car on the road, and now here they were in the shade of the tall rodeo fence, obviously enjoying old friendships and connections. I didn't know them personally, but I had heard of them for years and was curious. Doris and Madeline are sisters who, until his death recently, lived for parts of the year, at least, with their older brother Casimil Lulua at Tullin Ranch in the shadow of Tullin Mountain above Chilko Lake. Casimil was a long-time cowboy in the area, having worked for the Tatla Lake and C1 ranches, among others, and he was respected for his knowledge and competence. His sisters were noted for being the last of the older folks to go up into the Potato Mountains in late June or early July to dig spring beauty, otherwise known as Indian potatoes, when the lower alpine slopes were white with their flowers. They stopped going up there only a few years ago. Their mother, Eleene Lulua, older sister to Tommy and Emily, would likely have taken them and brother Cas up the old northeast trail over the shoulder of Tullin Mountain, into the alpine, when they were small children.

Eleene, who is remembered by some as a loquacious person, was a daughter of Jack Lulua, a man of the old days and old-time ways whose reputation has a tinge of the mysterious about it. Occasional stories come down to us from remote corners of the West Chilcotin plateau that include passing references to this man, wispy mentionings on the edges of discussions, never direct, never head-on, but drifting around as if somehow incidental and beyond acute description. They say he was an independent man who did and said what he wanted, a character who was known to play practical jokes and sing at the top of his voice as he rode along on his horse. They say he took crap from no one. Some say he claimed he was an eyewitness to the episode in 1864 at Murderer's Bar down the Homathko River, the main event of the Chilcotin War, where fourteen road builders were killed, some in their sleep, for their unwillingness to share their—probably limited—food supplies and for the threats and abusive acts by at least some members of the crew against Tsilqot'in people. Jack would have been a child then.

Emily Lulua Ekks. Photo courtesy of Sage Birchwater.

Like certain other old-time, backcountry folks—Chiwid, George Turner, Theodore Valleau, Neganie Guichon and Eagle Lake Henry,

129

Donald Ekks. Photo courtesy of Sage Birchwater.

to name several—Jack Lulua sounds as if he had that old wild in him in a way that is beyond our comprehension now. These were people raised in the hard bush world when life was mostly deprived, frequently short and rough, and basic survival was the goal. But the myth world would have been lively in those times, and the old stories, including the old myth stories, were presences to be heard and acknowledged. The times were slow and quiet enough that when the rocks and trees and rivers spoke, the people would hear and know something of what was being expressed. That was a world with layers and edges and core essences that few of us now, in these digitally urban, ungrounded times in which we find ourselves, could recognize or experience, let alone trust. Back then, if you hoped to endure, you'd best work hard and learn to pay full attention.

The Lulua sisters, Doris and Madeline, are Jack's granddaughters, of course, and have come directly from that old bush world of not so long ago. As the rodeo unfolded, I could see that Doris was wearing a pretty beaded choker necklace of her own making and was dressed up as if she was looking forward to the social gathering that evening. She was moving about, looking lean and energetic and a bit restless, her hair long and black "as a raven's wing," to echo Gerry Bracewell's description of Chiwid at Graveyard Springs. Madeline, the younger sister, a motionless, featureless figure in the shadow of the fence, was sitting and talking with a younger man, big and square-shouldered in a black shirt, his face partly hidden under the wide brim of his bright white cowboy hat.

The year following, I heard that Emily had gone down to bathe in Cochin Lake one day as she had done regularly for years. Later, Donald found her by the lake's edge, curled up and still, as if she had settled quietly down to sleep, something she might well have done after a warm-weather swim, only this time she was dead. She had lived for eighty-six years. And Donald died just two years after Emily in a small, mysterious fire in tall grass by the side of the highway on the outskirts of Tatla Lake. What on earth had come upon him in those last moments for such a strange event to occur? With Emily gone, was the hole in his life too deep to bear?

On the same day as Donald's departure from this Earth, Sage Birch-water had driven by him as he was walking in the opposite direction along the Chilcotin highway. After Sage heard the bad news, he berated himself for not turning his car around and driving back to offer a ride. Donald did not drive and was known to hitch rides in and out of Tatla for groceries at the general store or to attend church. As Sage writes, "It was a stormy, snow-buffeting, early spring day, in March or April. Donald was buttoned up against the weather, walking through the storm toward Tatla Lake Chapel where an afternoon potluck was to be served later in the day. He had a kilometre or so to go. I suppose I rationalized that church-goers would pick him up, and possibly they did ... Donald was walking purposefully westward into the wind."

NEW BURIALS AT BIG EAGLE LAKE

*Home is where the stones have not stopped breathing
and the light is still alive.*

"Breathing through the Feet:
An Autobiographical Meditation"
—Robert Bringhurst

IT WAS SAGE Birchwater who first told me that Donald Ekks and Emily Lulua Ekks had been buried in an old graveyard situated all by itself in a meadow on the edge of woods somewhere along the south side of Big Eagle Lake (otherwise known on maps and to the big world outside as Choelquoit Lake). Big Eagle lies approximately east-west between Chilko and Tatlayoko lakes. Lee Butler had also commented on the place. He described it as a small, fenced cemetery close to the southeast end of Big Eagle and mentioned that the old couple is interred there next to each other; Emily has her own grave house complete with windows and a little door. Sage had attended her funeral over there—in fact, he had given the eulogy—and he exclaimed to me that the setting is unusually beautiful and just about his favourite place in the world.

Naturally I was curious, and as I reflected on it over the winter of '06–'07, I felt a growing urge to see Donald and Emily's final resting stop for myself: my mental image of the place was too compelling. I had a feeling that, like Jack Lulua and others of the older generations, those two old folks stood for something ancient, fathomless and stark: old lives well lived and a way of life pretty much passed for good. I would not have wished for that way of living myself for a whole host of reasons, although in its isolation, frugality and basic simplicity there were hints of the old life in my own childhood bush years up the North Thompson Valley after the war. Since that time I have had a persistent inclination to observe and feel and understand aspects of the old country ways for myself, before we forget altogether that those old ways of being in and seeing the world even existed. The curse of our current times, parallel to the growing incapacity of society at large to comprehend rural land-based life, is our forgetting. Our greatest forgetting, generated from a half-millennium of rampant hubris, may be that we too are animals, albeit big-brained and complex, and an irrevocable part of nature.

My father grew up out in Sooke, west of Victoria, in difficult times and knew what it meant to grow your own food and hunt wild meat for the table. Consequently he had a basic appreciation and respect for country lives and for the importance of places and history, and he passed some of that sense down to my brothers and me. We grew up knowing something of where we came from, where we lived and how to survive there, and it is natural for us now to view this land we live in as, in part, our land, to the extent that any of us can claim a place at all. We three are rooted here; we do not see ourselves as baseless. The stories we heard and learned to tell are our stories. Some of those places we knew are fraught with myth, and we have a congruent need, those of us who are so called, to attempt to plumb and comprehend their mysteries and meaning. Therefore, while the old cemetery by Big Eagle Lake and the area around have been an integral part of indigenous life "since time immemorial," it is understand-able for any of us so inclined to view Donald and Emily's burial spot as a holy place; a place of significance, beauty and power; a place that merits our deepest acknowledgement and respect. This northwest ground we live and walk on, and drive over, is the great linchpin that binds all of us to here and transcends our differences. We are not disparate, although many of us in these times have come to believe, think and act as if we are.

To find that little cemetery in the wild I would need explicit directions, and so that same winter I asked Sage how far it was past the one-table

Looking to the southeast across the east end of Big Eagle Lake. Ts'yl-os looms in the background. Photo courtesy of John Schreiber.

Forestry campsite off the main road at the east end of Big Eagle Lake. Sage assured me it was "not far" and that I should "just follow the track" past the campsite and on down the lake.

I had been through the area fairly often and had camped at the site by the log corrals a number of times; it's the kind of campsite where you need to bring your own water. The setting is open, rolling grasslands interspersed with groves of poplar and lodgepole pine, and thick pine or spruce forest at higher elevations. In late May, golden balsamroot sun-flowers bloom on the long, open, sun-facing slopes overlooking the lake. They must be some of the most northerly balsamroot in all of British Columbia and, thus, the entire continent. Like most Forestry campsites in the Interior, this one is located at a place of old, even ancient, use, a crossroads, a deep place. It is not necessary to be psychic to feel it. The site is located where the old, now-defunct, wagon track running along the lake and swamp edges between Skinner Meadow and the Chilko River and Chilko Lake meets the more recent Forestry trunk road over higher ground from Tatla and Tatlayoko lakes. Short distances to the east are two important turnoffs: one road runs northeast down along the Chilko River all the slow, rocky, rooty way past Lava Canyon to the Newton Ranch on the old Chilcotin highway.

The second turnoff, a little farther south, passes over the Chilko River at Henry's Crossing, continuing on to Tsuniah Lake, and up Chilko Lake as far south as the west end of Nemaiah Valley and the stirring sight of snow-covered mountain peaks all around, close and in the long distance. The most imposing presence of all is Ts'yl-os (called Mount Tatlow on older maps), just south of Nemaiah. Some of the potholes on a dark, damp stretch of road at the western foot of Mount Nemaia are straight clay dirt, as big as swimming pools at runoff time or in wet weather, and just about as deep. You need to slide quickly into four-wheel drive to crawl into and out of them like some water-pushing amphibious machine.

Not far east, past the bridge over the Chilko, is Mountain House, where Eagle Lake Henry ranched and raised good horses, the best in his day, so they say. On the near side, closer to Big Eagle Lake and overlooking muskrat and beaver swamps along the river, is the cluster of three small houses, now abandoned, where generations of Luluas, including Emily's older brother Tommy, had lived. Tommy's son Henry was the last person to live there. This would have been old Jack Lulua's home territory as well.

Here and there through the meadows and poplar bottoms around the southeast end of Big Eagle Lake are fading signs of old camps: mossy, axe-cut stumps; grassed-in fire rings; tent poles; crude lean-to frames; a short wired-pole windbreak; a sawhorse still intact and standing; split firewood rotting back into the soil; tin cans flattened and rusted; the bottom of a galvanized washtub; old tether posts for horses out on the open flats. These signs were left over from an era before the bridging of the big river, when people travelled through the country by horse, wagon or on foot, and journeys were measured in time, tea-fires, sleeps or hay meadows, but not so much by miles. In those old slow days, time was flexible and distance was not. Now, internal combustion technology has largely overcome distance if you've got the cash for gas, the roads are clear and your truck motor is tuned up enough to get you home again. Now it's time that's rigid, fixed, trapped.

On a walk along the Big Eagle lake-edge one evening some years ago, the sun falling down behind the mountains in the far west above Tatlayoko Lake, I came upon a pair of wagon wheel rims, iron hoops of great diameter, head-high at least, hanging on a high branch in deep poplar brush not far from one of the old camps. They must surely have belonged to Eagle Lake Henry himself. He was noted not only for the quality of his stock and his business acumen, woods knowledge, accuracy with a rifle, and unpredictability, but also for the big wheels on his wagons, which were sufficiently tall that with good, skookum horses he could ford all but the highest water at the wide, gravelled shallows of the river crossing named after him. I reckoned the camp was about a day's wagon trip from Mountain House, and I wondered if Henry didn't stop at this location from time to time, a half century or more earlier, to change to or from regular-sized, or even rubber-tired, wheels for the rest of his journey.

I hung Henry's rims carefully in the half-hidden place where I had found them and was surprised the following year to rediscover them hanging off a fence post a short mile north along the end of the lake, not far from the old C1 Ranch line cabin, known in earlier times as "Jim Holt's cabin." Holt, who happened to be Lee Butler's step-grandfather, had cowboyed a while for the C1. The desiccated, dull-feathered body of an immature bald eagle lay in the collapsed remains of the original cabin; a larger, newer cabin, its interior recently trashed, stands not far away. In the short time since I first spotted the rims, someone had found and, for some unknown reason, moved them. What subtle currents occur on this Earth that allow those old rims to hang intact and undisturbed all those decades and then, soon after I dislodge them from their original hiding place, come to be so easily disconnected, dislocated and removed?

The desiccated, dull-feathered body of an immature bald eagle lay in the collapsed remains of the original cabin.

In mid-May of '07 I headed north for the Big Eagle Lake cemetery and those newly dug graves, armed with a few facts and a fantasy or two of what I might find when I reached the place. I was alone. I made my slow passage across the Chilcotin Plateau, spotting spring birds and checking out bird sloughs and old places along the way: Siwash (Anah) Lake above Alexis Creek, now drying up, and Chilanko Marsh out west; Ollie Knoll's well-built old two-storey house, alone and empty at the far end of the marsh; the traditional gathering site at Siwash Bridge up the Chilko River; and Tachadolier's old cabin and corral farther along the highway. These were all places I'd seen before, but each new visit to an old and lively place, especially at a different time of day or season, is a fresh experience. Each time I feel as if, once again, I "know the place for the first time." The light is never the same; the range of small, unique moments that compose each such experience is virtually infinite.

The afternoon I arrived was perfect and full of promise as fresh spring days nearly always are. The big lake was bright blue and calm; the poplars were greening; birds were flitting about, bold and half-crazy with life; my gas tank was close to full; there were two or three beer in the cooler; and my head was full of memories from past trips and historical references. I parked just past the Forestry site on a small rise and took time to absorb the long view down the lake. The ridges and mountains around and beyond were clear and shining; the snow line was low.

Big Eagle Lake was known for a short while as McLean's Lake, and these years I cannot look down the lake without remembering that the life of Donald McLean was brought to its abrupt (many would say timely) termination along its southern shore, in 1864. For his alleged cruelties, McLean was ambushed and shot in the final episode of the Chilcotin War. Now, each time I drive over the low divide from Tatlayoko and look out over the shimmering waters of Big Eagle, I visualize briefly what I imagine to be the event and place somewhere down there in that long, far distance. I have not actually seen the site.

I remembered that Charlie Skinner's horses used to run through this valley in great numbers; they grew more numerous, inbred and wild, and in his old age they got away from him. I've walked through the brush on the southern shore of Goosenob Lake, across the road from Big Eagle—about where he had built a rough corral to hold his horses—and found axe marks and twisted baling wire on standing tree trunks, old and black enough to have been made by him. Along the old low track west of Big Eagle Lake, on the edge of Skinner Meadow, his half-completed but carefully built and solid roadhouse still stands, with a spiky Engelmann spruce growing out of it now.

Marne and I camped in this place not long ago. That night the moon rose big and bright, and the trees at the meadow edges cast long shadows out onto the open grass. We were kept awake for a while, not only by what sounded like whole families of coyotes yipping and yowling, long and loud, in the woods across from our tent, informing us in no uncertain terms whose territory this was, but also by small flocks of ducks flying low over us from Big Eagle Lake, the sound of air whistling through wing feathers indicating most were goldeneyes. I concluded they were seeking calmer night waters on the much smaller Goosenob and Rosse lakes to the north. Pairs of conversing geese flew back and forth, seemingly barely above our tent, cackling small intimacies to each other as they passed. It was busy out there.

Marne was a little spooked by the coyotes and asked if I might "get out and do something to scare them away."

"Like what?" I replied. I was rather enjoying their nighttime yelling myself. I stepped gingerly out into the dew-wet grass and waved and shouted at them for a bit, and in good time the coyote choir quit.

I started up the Pathfinder again and picked my way in along the

The cemetery at Big Eagle Lake. Photo courtesy of John Schreiber.

track, which was at best two shallow, bumpy ruts in the rocky sod, to where I guessed the old burial place might be. The first quarter mile was the original road to Chilko Lake and points south. Johnny Blatchford's little signboard, pointing the way to his former outfit at the top end of Tsuniah Lake, was still there all these years later, nailed to its pine tree. After a false right turn close to the lakeshore on what I had hoped was old trail sign, and a walk-around to check for more track or trail, I retreated and veered inland past a pair of large white horses grazing peacefully on an open flat; they were tame but still had their winter hair, and they looked to me like an old matched team turned out for spring. I rounded a corner and there on the other side of a small, elevated clearing beyond a single massive boulder, a glacier-dropped erratic, was the cemetery, the place I'd been hearing about and imagining: a wire fence and gate against cattle, and a collection of grave-fence boards and crosses all the same shade of weathered grey. At the back, tall behind the last row of graves, stood a single dun-coloured cross.

The lake flashes a million bright reflections in the light of the dropping sun; a late-in-the-day breeze riffles the waters. The lake and the mountains behind look and feel like they have been here without change forever.

I parked and walked slowly over to unlatch the gate, noticing immediately that there were three new burial mounds on my right, the first two
topped with small, low, long-roofed grave houses. The nearest held the
temporal remains of Eliza William, who was born early in the twentieth
century and died in 2005, God rest her soul. Emily Lulua's house was next,
graced with plastic side windows to see in or out of, as Lee Butler had
indicated. Donald Ekks's mound of dug earth was close behind Emily's.
All three were festooned with a variety of offerings: wreaths and crosses
of plastic flowers (now fading), diminutive crosses, crucifixes, rosaries,

Donald Ekks's grave mound and crosses, and Emily Lulua's grave house.
Photo courtesy of John Schreiber.

a picture or two of Jesus, a dream-catcher, a model moose, a stuffed toy bear, small vases for flowers. Some of the artificial flowers were daisy-like and reminiscent of balsamroot sunflowers. Emily has a stout granite cross at the front of her house with the words *In Loving Memory of ?Inkel* embossed above her English names and dates. An image of a log raft, like one she fished from on Cochin Lake most likely, is situated to one side. Donald has an ornately shaped, pebbled cross in front of his burial spot, with the words *To the Man who went Home* inscribed on an embedded metal plate. Many of the polished pebbles are a jade shade of green. There is much care and faith demonstrated in this place.

After murmuring my own respects as deeply as I was able—the least I could do in the face of such solicitude—I walked slowly around the yard. Many of the graves were old; several had been surrounded by low, log grave houses or fences at one time; others were just shallow, grassed-in pits in the ground with no crosses, no names now, mostly child-sized. One grave had a tall figurine of Christ at the back. Another had two standing china Virgin Mary figurines among the aged plastic flowers; one had obviously fallen over and broken in pieces, and some careful person had gone to the trouble of gluing the pieces roughly, minus a couple of shards, back into place again. A group of intact, well-fenced, not-so-weathered graves was situated on the left closer to the gate; each site had its carved wooden cross. The inscription of one commemorated Tommy Lulua who, after a long and respected life, died in 1978. Near Tommy lay his brother Lashway and sister-in-law Mary Jane Lulua, daughter of Chiwid. Mary Jane's stone was reddish polished granite, identical to her husband Henry's, whose burial place was right beside hers. But Henry outlived his wife by twenty-four years.

I was at the back of the graveyard, bent over one of the older graves and peering to decipher the faint letters, made up of sets of small nail holes, that were etched on an ornately carved, sunburned wooden cross heeled over at a sharp—one might almost say "crazy"—angle, exactly the same angle as the picket enclosure in front of it. The letters were coalescing dimly into my conscious mind as *Jack Lulua* when I heard what sounded like a combination deep cough and grunt—very loud—then another and another and another. I looked up fast and there, just across the meadow from me, about six, maybe eight, seconds away, were two good-sized grizzly bears, both a rich chocolate brown with undershades of off-red. One was up on two legs, attempting to understand exactly what I was about; the other, back turned, seemingly unconcerned, was intent on some herbal delicacy he/she had discovered. On the right, trotting keenly along the edge of the buckbrush, came two more large bears, both the same shade of red-brown as the first pair. This was obviously a family group. The last bear, judging by her great size and demeanour, had to be Mum. The three cubs, each larger than the average black bear, looked the right size to be three-year-olds and not long from setting out on their own. Mother and number three cub joined right in on the huffing and puffing, coughing and grunting. She was pacing back and forth, obviously alarmed and trying to determine the best line of action. The group, except for the preoccupied number two cub, was accelerating the frequency and volume of its chorus of coughs; Mama's nervousness was not helping.

I was thinking I should maybe sidle slowly over toward my car and stand near it, just in case. Unfortunately, the vehicle was somewhat in front of me, and my slow forward walking, meant to be casual and unthreatening, only served to incite Mum's coughing and pacing. I reached the car at the same moment that Mama chose finally to make her considered decision to pull the pin and leave. Off they went at a gallop, minus the distracted one, crashing and coughing into the brush; the last of Mama's offspring looked up to see her family gone and chugged off to join them. I was abruptly alone, but for the grazing white horses over on the flats. The place was completely silent. It would have been better to simply stand there by old Jack's tomb and watch.

It turned out to be a good year for grizzly bear family contacts. In August at Gun Creek, out of Gold Bridge, Marne and I walked by a small mother and skookum young cub focused on a generous roadside saskatoon berry crop two or three hundred yards down from Warren and Casie Menhinick's barn, sheds and horse corrals. That particular bear mother was known to den just a quarter mile away, likely using the Menhinicks' place as cover from big male bears. Casie had shooed her off from their home place several times, and I had seen tracks in the dust at the side of the road but chose to say nothing to Marne. My intention was to be reassuring, but my flippant salutation, "Hi, kids," not only lacked respect but had an unintended edge and did not improve Mama's response. She moved her big grizzly head from side to side, trying to get a fix on the smartass out on the road. I changed my tune instantly to a much more polite and acknowledging tone; Mother Grizzly made one of those quick, bear eye-contacts with me, learned in an instant what she needed to know, turned and, followed by junior, ambled off into the brush to put some distance between us. For me, this incident was a real demonstration of the power of voice tone, body language and attitude. Bears, like all large predators, are smart and detect subtle messages, intended and unintended. They smell us. As Alberta bear man and legend Andy Russell, now deceased, declared: "When you carry the gun, you carry the gun mentality."

When you carry the gun, you carry the gun mentality.

Grizzly bear family. Photo courtesy of Larry Travis Raincoast Images, and Jane Woodland & Chris Genovali: Raincoast Conservation Foundation.

Later in August, Don Brooks and I drove out to a potential campsite on the lower Tchaikazan River in that wild country south of Ts'yl-os and Nemaiah Valley, near the top end of Taseko Lake. We got out quickly, walked over to the bank to scan the river and sighted a brown mother grizzly and two cubs, probably three-year-olds, below us, all a good size and obviously not alarmed as they quietly and elegantly walked away through the bear-high willow brush, out of sight. They must have heard our car doors close. We were touched by their dignity and the good woods manners that so characterized the whole brief episode.

As much as any animal species out here in the west, grizzly bears epitomize wild. Their presence generates our most complete attention.

When the signs indicate that bears are around, I become immediately cautious, and an instant balancing seems to occur, a subtle equilibrium between my consciousness and that usually unseen, powerfully wild presence out there in the woods somewhere. My innate response is not fear so much as sharp-edged alertness, pure acuity of attention; I am aware that if the sign is fresh, the grizzly is, in all likelihood, aware of my presence. At some level, if the animal is not too long gone, it is as if our respective consciousnesses come together briefly. In this most delicate of equations, I have experienced, at times, a state of clarity and beauty, and a sense that this larger awareness I am a part of is a lively entity unto itself.

That evening after I visited the Big Eagle Lake cemetery, as I made my way over to Iris Moore and Dennis Redford's place at Tatlayoko Lake, I was feeling the fullness and sharpness of life. The sun was setting, the sky clear, the ridge edges fine, and I found myself nodding and quietly calling out to the mountains as I scanned and recognized them: Mount Nemaia and the long, snowy, no-name ridge on the near side of Tsuniah Lake; Tullin Mountain over Chilko Lake and, to the west, the two converging ridges that comprise the Potato Mountains; then little Mount Skinner and shadowy, rock-faced Niut Mountain (Eniyud) on the far side of Tatlayoko behind. Beyond Niut, over West Branch, Whitesaddle and Blackhorn loomed sharp-edged, snow-covered, dark. Razorback was hidden, out of sight. I said a respectful hello to them all. As I continued driving, I glanced in the car mirror, spotted Ts'yl-os in the far distance behind me, high over Nemaiah Valley, and proffered his reflected, much-reduced, image a cautious nod and wave, not too long, not too slight.

I reached the cabin, cooked a quick supper and, as night descended, settled in by the big window to look out at Eniyud. On the other side of the glass, rufous hummingbirds hovered at the sugar-water feeder or took time from feeding to ferociously drive newcomers out of the territory, darting faster than I could track them.

For over an hour I sat absorbing Eniyud's craggy silhouette, dark across the water, with her angular offspring gathered around her, their forms fading into the blackening sky. The lake transmuted slowly to silver. After a time, but for snow ridges and patches gleaming, Eniyud was just a great, hard-edged shape in the gloom. Somewhere back in myth time, after a stormy marriage it seems, she separated from her consort, Ts'yl-os, over above Nemaiah, and ran off to Tatlayoko with most of the children, leaving the baby with him and, incidentally, scattering wild potato corms as she went. At some time in the process, the pair turned to rock. The myth stories suggest both personages were moody and mean—and are still apparently, so people say. We are advised to choose our thoughts and words carefully and not stare or point; lack of restraint and disrespect is risky. I have learned over time that to be in the company of gods, or even god-like mountains, demands mindfulness. How does a mountain express itself under trying or unmannerly circumstances? And do we want to be around to find out? I retired to the warmth of my down sleeping bag.

All night long, in the red osier dogwoods and willows around the open outhouse behind the cabin, a pygmy owl calls "hoo, hoo, hoo, hoo …," like slow falling water drops. Each (too frequent) time I wake and turn over, "hoo, hoo, hoo, hoo." The sound is oddly intimate, unpredictably musical.

This last May I travelled up into that Big Eagle Lake country alone again, and on a mission. I needed to be by myself for a while, up there in some of those beautiful places I love or have not yet seen, and quietly listen to my true heart-mind. I'd not done a lone trip the previous year and was feeling the lack. I'd heard the news that Casimil Lulua, brother to Doris and Madeline, had departed this Earth and been buried at Big Eagle, and I was

Ts'yl-os presiding over Tsoloss Ridge and Nemaiah Valley. Photo courtesy of John Schreiber.

inclined to feel the out-of-time atmosphere of that old cemetery again, view his new gravesite, sharpen up my bush senses a little and experience the liveliness of another early spring in Chilcotin land. Perhaps I'd find the conclusion to this story. In any event, I was sure, one way or another, that happenings out there would unfold as seamlessly and appropriately as they should.

I came up through the Fraser Canyon from Hope, and at Lillooet chose the slow, wild, West Fraser River route north to Watson Bar, scaring up black bears and moose at the roadside, and counting wintering deer by the dozens on the low, green flats below me as I drove. I slept that night in the back of the Pathfinder at Big Bar and crossed over on the reaction ferry to the east side the following morning. After stopping with my friends Karen and Don Logan at Clinton and Sage Birchwater in Williams Lake, and after a couple of good day walks—the first with Don; the second with Sage down into Stranger Wycott's old place up Churn Creek—I turned west and began my usual solo slow-drift across the plateau. On such a trip I travel casually, glassing the slopes and swamps, noting the expansion of the mountain pine beetle damage, checking out bighorn sheep at Deer Park on the Fraser, sighting several pairs of courting sandhill cranes at Anahim's Meadows and a fox hunting in tall grass by the road past Redstone. Foxes are strategic creatures, and this one was not only using the noise and motion of passing traffic as cover (a phenomenon I have observed several times) but was also building up a small stockpile of dead mouse bits at the road edge—to take back to the den, I expect. I spent an evening watching and listening to birds and coyotes, the usual spring mayhem, at a couple of large ponds up behind Alexis Creek. The following morning, after I checked out a diligent sapsucker that had quietly, almost secretively, tapped all night at a nest hole in the making in a poplar snag nearby, and after a slow wander, I packed up and wound my way back onto Highway 20 and points farther west.

On a side trip south, some distance off the main road, I got a good, extended look at a lanky, near-black wolf sizing up a bunch of Black Angus yearlings below the track by the smallest of the Goose Lakes above Wycott's place. I had been alerted by the sight of the cattle and a flock of puddle ducks all pointedly staring at something in willow brush at the pond edge, each critter motionless and on guard.

I stop to sit and watch too, and after two or three minutes out trots a wolf, high-tailed and rangy. The animal pauses to give us all a slow, deliberate assessment—first the cattle, then me—before loping casually off into the bush.

As so often happens with wild creatures, it appeared that my stopping stirred this wolf to modify its strategy and leave. Certainly any opportunities created by surprise were gone. Earlier, I had seen much oldish wolf scat, full of bone chips and deer hair and way too large to be coyote, along a section of grown-in wagon track in a little valley between Augustine's Meadow, on Little Gaspard Creek, and Blackwater (China) Lake. I thought that route might well be a section of the old Empire Valley–Chilcotin Trail. Wolves had been using it as a throughway the previous winter, and probably a denning location in the spring.

A day or two later, out west, as I crossed the open, sunflower slopes on my way to the Forestry site at Big Eagle Lake, I spied Ts'yl-os in the far distance, partially covered by a layer of white clouds but still dwarfing the peaks half-hidden behind him on the far side of Nemaiah. I've noticed frequently that no matter which valley in the area I traverse, Ts'yl-os is peeking over some ridge, watching. I nodded briefly, as usual. The weather was shifting; the sky in the west was clearing, the ridge lines were turning sharp, and late afternoon sunlight was slanting in from over by Tatlayoko. The arrow-shaped leaves of young balsamroot plants were showing, and the sunny gold of their flowers would soon gleam up here at the northern limits of their range. Someone down near the lake was pushing cattle: a few moving dots in a line on the landscape pointed in the direction of the open flats in front of the graveyard. On the track into the cemetery later, I had to nudge my slow way through a couple of dozen Herefords—calves, big mothers and a few yearlings now bunched up in front of me—to reach that particular meadow in the corner with its sharp-edged boulder the size of a small cabin, and the fenced-in grave places past it.

The more I witness that great, fractured erratic—its edges broken, not much worn—the more it makes itself felt, and the more I sense it stands for something. It came out of the mantle of the Earth from not far away, it has certain power, and I'm realizing that it may be the reason the graveyard is situated in this meadow here, and not somewhere else. I recall the historic and mythic importance of other stony eminences in the territory: Ts'yl-os, Eniyud high over Tatlayoko Lake, the great Mount Waddington in the core of the Coast Range, the big rock-painting boulder in the pines on the far side of

Casimil Lulua's gravesite at Big Eagle Lake. Photo courtesy of John Schreiber.

the snake fence near Towdystan, and two hollow volcanic stone erratics, known as "Coyote's sweat-houses," in a meadow south of Stone Reserve by the road to Nemaiah. In an edition of *Hoofprints*, Lou Haynes relates a story told to him by Lashway Lulua of a canoe-shaped rock dropped somewhere along the old track to Skinner Meadow, left there supposedly by two myth-time ravens.

Just inside the cemetery gate, the fence boards and posts around Casimil Lulua's new grave mound were fresh, bright and substantial, and the letters of the commemoration on his new cross were carefully and sharply carved in small neat letters, much like the delicate little letters painted on the sign for Tullin Ranch on the road to Chilko Lake. I noticed that his first name was spelled "Casimer," not "Casimil" or "Cas" as he was mostly known. I took a slow, deliberate walk around the place, standing and recognizing each of the more familiar individuals—Casimil(er), Eliza William, Emily Lulua and Donald Ekks, Jack Lulua, Tommy Lulua and Lashway Lulua, next to Tommy, Mary Jane and Henry—leaving a tiny offering of trail mix and a few acknowledging words at each place. I wished I'd brought tobacco. The plastic flowers on Casimil's mound were still colourful, and other offerings featured reminders of his life as a cowboy: two bucking broncos, a model cowboy boot and a tiny saddle. The tall cross with the shellac peeling off it at the back of the graveyard had fallen over in the winter, smashing several of Jack Lulua's grave pickets. I'm guessing old Jack would have had a good laugh.

I stopped for a bit to lean on a fence post and gaze out across the meadow to where grizzly mother and her three big chocolate-brown cubs had been and remembered my brief but intense meeting with them two springs earlier. All was still out there on this evening. As always, in the back, the mountains were just there, seemingly unmoving, exuding power.

The next morning at the Forestry site was sunny, but there was a solid layer of ice in the water jug; the warm season was only just beginning.

A ruffed grouse, with boundless stamina, had thumped all night. Pairs of amorous sapsuckers and yellow-rumped warblers chased each other through the willows, and geese and a couple of loons, heavy and low, flew by between lakes. I wondered how those loons, most ancient of birds, deep-diving helpers to the northern creator gods, could lift themselves enough off the waters to fly. After a fast breakfast I sat a little, warming in the sun and letting the stillness of this great lonely land seep into my bones. At one point my thoughts slowed long enough for me to mutter to myself, "Let go and just be." The words had an impact, and the immediate Eagle Lake world around me seemed to shift and slow a little; details sharpened.

A muddy pickup truck in a hurry banged down the track in the direction of the graveyard and the grazing cattle, and I raised my hand for a brief wave the way we do on back roads in rural places. The driver obligingly returned my wave, but the gesture struck me as reluctant.

Two undetermined grassland-type sparrows, probably Savannahs, played coy on an orange lichen-topped rock: he chased, wings displayed handsomely, tail dragging; she demurred. He appeared to give up the pursuit; she gave him pecks and eye blinks, and the male resumed the chase all over again. And I watched the dance from twenty feet away.

I decided to go for a wander down the track for another look at the old camps in the poplar bottoms along the way and to enjoy the morning. I could hear cows bawling, dutifully informing their offspring of their whereabouts. I'd only walked a few minutes when a slow line of cows and calves appeared through a strip of trees below me, pushed by the pickup driver in her truck and a diminutive elderly lady in chaps, on foot, leading a fine, saddled, buckskin horse. An enthusiastic cow dog was helping out by heading off strays. I realized these two cow herders were the Lulua sisters themselves, from Tullin Ranch: Doris the driver and Madeline with the horse. Madeline had obviously ridden over on the old track from Chilko Lake. I took considerable care to circle up the grassy slope above and around the moving stock so as not to upset them any more than they already were. The animals clearly preferred to be back grazing on the newly greened flats over near the graveyard.

Doris called out from the truck to inform me in firm, sharp-voiced terms that their animals had not seen people on foot much and were easily spooked. She sounded nervous. The dog came by to give me a quick, good-natured inspection.

Casimil Lulua and Doris Lulua. Photo courtesy of Sage Birchwater.

I continued walking along the edge of the trees, noting the old campsites and various hints of old occupation, and heard a bird song, thrush-like

The Lulua sisters' cattle herd on the move at Big Eagle Lake. Tullin Mountain is in the background. Photo courtesy of John Schreiber.

in its full bell tones and sequence, ringing out of the low timber ahead of me. A veery or hermit thrush, I thought, not the rising flute-like song of a Swainson's thrush, and definitely not a robin. The bird sang again, twice, with a good pause between, clear in the morning quiet, and slightly haunting. Its song had that out-there-in-the-woods-all-alone feel.

I took advantage of a rough cow trail for a bit, then branched off to pick my way up a little brushy hump, a gravelly micro-esker of sorts. On the knoll top I came upon a group of ancient kekuli holes, closely bunched and partially overgrown with wild roses and stubby poplar shoots. Sometimes when you don't go looking for pithouse holes, you find them. I could scarcely believe my good fortune to be in this spot at this time. As I beheld the kekulis in their setting, here in this anonymous piece of bush, and absorbed the fineness of the moment, I got the small shivers and spinal tingling that seem often to measure connectedness and the power of intrinsic truth. In these instances, I am free to know that the world is aware and watching. The world is always watching, as we make our mistakes or get the balances as truly as we can, our feet on the ground, living and learning. Those mother bears I'd seen were watchful too in their different, ursine ways, and they were not alone. Virtually all mamas are watchful in this world; that is their inherent inclination and vocation, springing from deep within themselves. I have to remind myself constantly that, to the extent we can see at all, we can know this watching if we let go, accept possibilities and keep our eyes, ears, mind and heart open.

There were six pits on this knoll by Big Eagle Lake, in a tight L configuration. The largest three were each about fifteen feet across and six feet deep. Some pits were semi-filled and brushed-in; the others were deeper and looked to have been inhabited in more recent times. People lived their lives here, for centuries most likely, in all those old, tough, subtle, survival ways. Pithouses were winter houses, and with the lake edge only a hundred yards away at the high-water mark, I could picture winter ice-fishing out there. Possibly the older folks who paused at the old campsites nearby were passing through, in part, to stay connected to where and who they came from, and to who they still were. That would have been a natural thing to do back then, especially if the times were trying.

As I made my own way away from the kekuli place, I half-heard two or three rich, single-note thrush calls, slightly echoey in the trees; in another minute or two, a bird, a thrush, presented itself openly and easily on the sunlit bare branch of a spindly poplar just a few feet in front of me. This was a fairly rare event for me: a bright, unhurried look, enough to see the distinctly spotted white breast of a hermit thrush, normally a secretive creature. We hear their one-noted, crystal bell-call, in deep woods typically, but we don't see them easily, hence the aptness of their name.

On the way out, having reached my vehicle, I passed by the Lulua sisters sitting on a tarp or blanket just down from the corrals. They had herded their cows into the pens and now were resting and talking. Doris's hair was still as black as a raven's wing. Madeline's dark-maned buckskin, its bridle hanging from the saddle horn, was head down, grazing—a contented horse I expect. The dog lay comfortably on guard close by. I waved, and this time it was Madeline who responded with a small impassive wave of her own. I drove away and took the turn left at the corner for Tatla Lake.

At a point a short quarter mile up the road across the open slopes above Big Eagle, I was suddenly startled to see, boiling up from below the road edge in front of me, three large, roly-poly grizzly bears, quite close, all similarly silver-tipped, the sun shining off their dark pelage. I got a clear, instant look at one round, dished-in, mother grizzly face, intent, looking back, protecting. There was a great, three-humped, surging movement—pure raw bear power—and they were gone, up the hill and into spruce timber: a bear mother and her two large, nearly full-grown cubs. Nothing more to see; not a branch moving; no sign of them at all, except tracks in the dust at the side of the road if I'd thought to stop and step out to check. I was too engrossed staring up the slope, looking for any last possible intimations of movement. Not a sign. Nothing.

LARRY EMILE'S DRUM

There are some places around this country
where we pray.

—Percy Rosette

FOR ME, THE story of Larry Emile's drum begins on a basalt knoll out past Gang Ranch on the west side of the Fraser River; I was camped there briefly in mid-May 2010. For Larry, who shot the deer, processed the hide, fashioned a drum from it, then made a gift of that newly made drum to me out at Big Meadow, and for Mildred Kalelest, Phil Anderson and the others, this story of land and place began much earlier, maybe two centuries ago.

The weather had been cool, with only patches of sun. The spring birds were late, grass was slow greening and, except close to the Fraser, the poplars, willows and cottonwoods were not yet in leaf. I had been out walking and linking up sections of a near-forgotten wagon track between Blackwater (China) Lake and William "Stranger" Wycott's second pre-emption, from 1884—this one in the name of his eldest son, Tom—over on a section of Gaspard Creek. (Stranger Wycott's main property was down near Wycott Flats above Churn Creek.) This old route is grown in and reduced to cow trails now, but it had been in use long before logging

Basalt knoll above William's Meadow west of Gang Ranch. Photo courtesy of Marne St. Claire.

trunk roads were superimposed upon the country. I discovered that this particular track split only a mile or so south of where I was camped. One branch continued south past a small, obscure pre-emption near a swampy lake to Big Meadow and the Gang Ranch cow camp and corrals there; another, the main stem I think, ran across country to Gaspard Lake and, eventually, to Hungry Valley far to the southwest.

One May earlier, I had walked through a nearby valley by a little lake named Snake and found much wolf sign: tracks, scattered bones, partially chewed hides, and numerous scat piles full of jagged bone chips and deer hair. The following July, from that same basalt bluff where Marne and I were camped, we heard wolves howling at dusk, in the dark past midnight, and again at the first light of dawn. Hearing both the long, low moans of adults and pup yips, we were curious about the likelihood of a den over there somewhere. I suspect the animals were very aware that we were in their territory.

Now, a year later, on a wander along the marginally visible old track through that same valley, I found no new signs of wolf existence at all. There was only last year's poop, dried or moldy, and much rather conspicuous, almost showy, coyote sign, fresh, and right close to the older shit of their larger cousins, a sure indication that the wolves had vacated the place. Yet across the area in general, I was spotting parts of many deer skeletons, at least one Black Angus yearling carcass, and moose bones and hide, all fairly fresh and thoroughly stripped, all likely wolf-kills.

I was pondering all of this, and eating the light supper I'd cooked at the back of my Pathfinder, when I heard the sound of cars and spotted dust rising along the gravel trunk road below me. I had heard little traffic that day, though earlier I did note an especially red red-tailed hawk circling off the knoll's steep side and calling its so-familiar burry call, to scare up small prey-critters down in last year's dead grass, I believe. I'd seen the bird make the same purposeful circles the day before, even landing on the same lookout treetop. I was not used to looking down from above on a raptor hunting. It seemed to have come out from the cliff face below me both days, and I thought there must be a nest there. From a distance I'd seen pale guano streaks down the rock.

One of the approaching vehicles rattled and banged badly. The high knoll I was on had the look and feel of an aboriginal special place; there was a substantial campsite down the grassy backslope, lightly and neatly used, with long tent poles, a privy, and a tended gravesite and cross off to one side. The inscription read *Paul Rosette 1930*, and in rough letters beneath *son of Joe Rosette*. I'd heard talk of other graves somewhere down along the expansive meadow below, so I was fairly sure the vehicles would turn up onto the knoll.

I was standing, waiting, and sure enough a white pickup, front bumper askew, ground into sight and pulled up the track to the top of the slope beside me.

Paul Rosette's burial place. Photo courtesy of Marne St. Claire.

"How ya doing?" the friendly-faced driver greeted me.

"Sleepy, but good," I replied. He smiled, and we began talking. It turned out he was Larry Emile from Canoe Creek, and he'd cowboyed here and there, including Gang Ranch and Empire Valley Ranch south of Churn Creek. His young grandson Vincent was sitting on the front seat beside him.

"Did you hear us coming in?"

"You bet," I said, "about an hour and a half ago." That was good for a chuckle.

The second car arrived and out popped Phil Anderson, his wife Mildred Kalelest and their two lively grandchildren, Challon and Regan, from up Canoe Creek Valley. We recognized each other right off. I'd talked with Mildred the year before at Alkali Lake (Esk'et) at a combined AA roundup and elders gathering that included a public launch of Lorne Dufour's new book *Jacob's Prayer*. Lorne's story, a long, sad and heroic one, was set at Esk'et, at nearby Alkali Lake Ranch, and by and on the lake itself.

Mildred (whose surname, not uncommon in the Cariboo–Chilcotin, is also spelled Kalalest, Kalelse or Kala'llst, varying from branch to branch in the family) is interested in tracking the history and old ways of her culture and had been enthusiastically studying James Teit's book on the Secwepemc (Shuswap) people. This extensive work consists of a great range of information, old stories and details of tribal boundaries and pre-contact village sites, collected in their own language from Secwepemc elders and compiled by the great lay anthropologist from Spence's Bridge over a century ago. Teit was working for the Jesup North Pacific Expedition, an anthropological investigation of Siberia, Alaska, and Canada's northwest coast, and was directed and edited by Franz Boas, the expedition's scientific leader. Mildred and I shared a sense of the importance of

Teit's Shuswap writings. I had read in Teit that a certain Kalle'llst was in fact Coyote's son, and he is featured in at least one of Teit's many Coyote-story translations. Kalle'llst's existence back in myth time raises the possibility that Mildred and her relatives are, in some way, descended from that primeval trickster figure.

At that same gathering, I talked in detail with Irvine Johnson, another James Teit proponent, who was raised at Esk'et and whose great-grand-father, Sixwi'lexken, had been an unusually knowledgeable and articulate source for Teit on his extended pack trip to Canoe and Dog creeks in 1900. Irvine, a youngish elder himself, had been told those same old stories in detail, year after year, by his grandfather as they walked back and forth from their summer camps. I asked Irvine if Teit got the stories right. He looked me in the face and said, "Word for word." I'm still in awe.

I had met Phil Anderson later, when I dropped by their home up Canoe Creek to sell them a copy of my book, *Stranger Wycott's Place*. I'd read about Phil's father, Davey, a man of character and great physical strength, in Don Logan's and Hillary Place's Dog Creek books.

Now Phil explained that they were on their way to do a wilderness campout with the kids, either out at West Churn Creek or Big Meadow, daylight permitting. He had been busy preparing for a similar backcountry trip when I'd met him the summer before. I told them I was headed out that same trunk road myself to see if the winter's snow had melted enough to allow me to reach Beaver (Lone) Valley at the back end of Gang Ranch range. Don Brooks and I thought there might be some good walks along the ridges out there for our next annual August trip, and I wanted to check them out and size up a possible campsite as well. It would be a slow drive south on that long road, wet and slick from runoff.

Larry confirmed my sense that this basalt hump was indeed a place of significance and that they had come by to pay their respects. He said they always stopped to pay tribute. They'd been taught that from the beginning by his Rosette relatives, who were from this part of the country; in fact, they would meet up with his uncle, Percy Rosette, and Percy's partner, Julia Gilpin, later that evening. Did I know of Percy? Did I know that he'd been involved at the Gustafsen Lake standoff between the RCMP and aboriginal protestors over land use rights and claims? In fact, I did remember his photo in the newspapers at the time. Percy was the one who got the bullet in the leg, and an electronic ankle bracelet later. Larry said he hadn't changed much. It was clear from the tone of his voice that Percy was somebody significant. At one point he smiled and exclaimed in a low voice to no one in particular "Percy, Percy, Percy," as if he was glad to be seeing him again. I would hear a number of quiet, but substantive, observations and questions from Larry. His comments were lightly delivered and easy to miss. Our discussion flowed smoothly like the words of a mutually sung song.

Some Secwepemc people had lived on the west side of the Fraser River in pre-contact times, not only around this and adjacent valleys, but out west as far as the Big Creek drainage. Some say farther still, although I suppose folks in Tsilhqot'in (Chilcotin) country would differ on that point. Perhaps some traditional territories overlapped. There were old Secwepemc village sites on the lower Chilcotin River and in Empire Valley. Diseases hit the Canyon and Empire Valley peoples early and hard, and most survivors moved across to villages and relatives on the east side of the

> *The old, sun-blackened Kalalest ranch buildings still stand, and there is a little graveyard just around the corner. Most of the graves are child-sized.*

165

river. However, members of the Rosette and Alex Kalalest families continued to live on in the area until recent times. Rosettes have cowboyed for
Gang Ranch for generations, and Alex Kalalest and Joe Kala'llst before
him had been independent cattle ranchers up Gaspard Creek around
where Gaspard Camp is now. The old, sun-blackened Kalalest ranch
buildings still stand, and there is a little graveyard just around the corner,
with concrete grave markers and a long view down the valley. Most of the
graves are child-sized.

We talked about this place, this columnar basalt extrusion, we
were standing on. Larry told me the name of the bluff is *Neech-help*
(approximately); he sounded it out carefully, but I still struggled with the
pronunciation. This would have been the term used by all those Rosettes,
relatives and ancestors, who lived on or near these meadows. Some quality in this place, reflected in the name *Neech-help*, would have directed
and allowed for Paul Rosette, son of Joe Rosette, to be buried up here on
the edge of the clearing. Joe was father to Percy Rosette as well, so Paul
and Percy were brothers. This area had, in effect, belonged to them all,
and Paul Rosette had died back into it early.

Phil, Larry, their grandchildren and I made our way over to the bluff
edge. Larry stopped to point out some low plant species in the rocks,
and we admired the view. I said I'd heard there were graves down there,
possibly in the vicinity of the old, recently burned-out cow-camp cabin
site and corrals farther down the meadow. Larry and Phil both said no,
the graves were located on the far side of the creek above the big bend in
the now grassed-in irrigation ditch. Larry pointed over my shoulder with
a small stick to show exactly where. There were fire-blackened, beetle-
killed lodgepole pines and poplar saplings on the slopes behind.

Later, after I had met him, I heard Percy Rosette say, almost incidentally: "There are some places around this country where we pray." Again, the conversation was a flowing thing, and Percy's words were on the edge of my hearing and understanding. I was intrigued by his statement, and I realized that *Neech-help* was likely such a place. When I asked Larry the meaning of *Neech-help*, he was vague; I suspect words are hard to find for the true meaning of the place. The English word "sacred," in its current rather two-dimensional, hard-edged and sometimes cliched usage, is probably not sufficiently refined to

The view north down William's Meadow. Photo courtesy of Marne St. Claire.

describe the supreme subtlety of these wild, lively places that abound out here and across the province. However, I sense that these are locations where connections occur. Such places, quietly existing, seem to inspire silence, deference, perhaps even something akin to love, and certainly deep attachment; we may find ourselves opening enough to truly know and accept that we are only ever a modest part of this great and infinitely complex whole that surrounds and includes us. In such a heart-place, we might well feel called upon to pray.

Larry and I carried on talking, comparing notes on a wide range of backcountry places. There is a certain deep pleasure in recalling old wild places with fellow wanderers, seekers, searchers of new country or new angles on old country, people you are sure have experienced and know wild.

I had explored, by horse and on foot, some of those good old hunting and prospectors' trails in the South Chilcotin Mountains.

Larry asked if I'd seen the big hole out in the mountains at the head of Lost (Dash Creek) Valley. I told him I didn't know that part of the country at all, but I've been curious to get over there to see the area. That big hole must be powerful to behold. He said that when he'd worked for Empire Valley Ranch, he packed up a saddle horse and took some days to ride over into the upper Taseko River country. He mentioned finding old caribou bones there; caribou are long, long gone from that land now. I said I'd been through there a bit, and over a couple of decades Don Brooks and I had explored, by horse and on foot, some of those good old hunting and prospectors' trails in the South Chilcotin Mountains, including especially the high Chilcotin Trail over Warner Pass. He asked if that big cabin was still in use at Trigger Lake, below Deer Pass. I replied that it was part of Menhinick's guiding outfit out of Gold Bridge; Warren now, and his father Barry before him, have used it for years.

At one point Larry exclaimed "So you like to walk, eh!"

I nodded yes and told him that I'd been down walking below China Lake to see if there were any old tracks into Wycott's place from there. In fact, I was out walking that afternoon, looking for new wolf sign in the little valley past Augustine's Meadow where the old wagon road used to run; I'd been down there the previous spring looking for signs of animal and old human life. Larry figured the wolves would have moved on through by now.

Phil Anderson announced that the elders and youth gathering, formerly held at Graveyard Valley in the vicinity of the old graves site up there, would take place at Mud Lakes off lower Relay Creek this year, July 4 to 18. There was an implicit invitation in his statement. Getting into Graveyard had taken a lot of time, effort and hassle, and involved trucking horses partway in on a poor piece of road. He said that he and Larry had been designated elders so that they might do the skin, gut and dress a fresh deer carcass demonstration for the young people this year. Both he and Larry smiled wryly as he spoke.

"What's it like now that you're elders?" I asked, as if we didn't know already.

Mildred, who doesn't appear to miss much, knew I was friends with Don and Karen Logan over at Clinton. Don has put together and self-published two fine collections of brief histories of local settler and aboriginal families at and around Big Bar Mountain (above Big Bar Creek) and Dog Creek, respectively. Both books have sold well throughout Cariboo country, and both include many samples from the sizable and unique collection of historic photos Don had gathered over the years. He and Mildred had talked about his current book on notable aboriginal and rancher folks at Canoe Creek, most especially the several generations of the Koster family, who owned and maintained the classic Canoe Creek Ranch (otherwise known as BC Cattle Company) on lower Canoe Creek. Now she asked if I knew how the project was going.

I gave her the new news that Don had finally completed the book, and that I found it to be fascinating, in part because of the extensive gallery of old personal photos from the Canoe Creek past. Several elder-ladies had entrusted their family pictures to him to duplicate, relying on his long-established reputation for their return. However, he'd only printed four copies this time. Don has been dealing with health problems which were absorbing his attention, and the project turned out to be more expensive than expected. The enterprise had become too much like work.

Because of our friendship and mutual interest in local history, Don had generously given me a copy, personally dedicated to Marne and me; I retrieved it from the car for Mildred to see. She was soon down on hands and knees on the grass, poring intently through the book, turning pages, recognizing faces and incidents, comparing names and relatives, with Phil and Larry standing and peering close behind her. The grandchildren played not far away.

The evening light was waning and it was time for the Canoe Creek crew to move on. Larry, Mildred and Phil were generous in parting. "It was great to see you," Mildred said, and Larry made sure I knew to drop by their camp for coffee next morning. As they started to drive away, I felt a quick impulse to send them off with something, as if I was now part of some kind of gift exchange. I raced to grab a small bag of Marne's home-made chocolate chip cookies from my food box, and passed it through the car window to Mildred, who seemed a bit startled. I knew the kids would enjoy them.

The next morning, after downing a cup of instant coffee and a bowl of cereal, and stowing my stuff, I climbed into the Pathfinder and drove out onto the gravel road headed southward for Big Meadow and points beyond. Deer were only just starting to move up from their low-elevation wintering grounds closer to the Fraser, but I spotted moose, including some, for the third year in a row, by that swampy, unnamed lake below

Clear-cuts in the foreground with cloud-enshrouded Red Mountain in the back. Photo courtesy of John Schreiber.

the road—a mother and last year's calf this time, casually high-stepping it across the wet bog edge to get out of eyeshot.

Farther along, at the top of a long hill, there is a turnout where a traveller might stop, if inclined, to scan the surrounding country. The panorama demands it: the wide swamp at the core of Big Meadow spreads out in front, with the low mountains at the heads of West Churn Creek, and Lost and Lone valleys to the southwest; the deep defile in the east that is Churn Creek winding its way out of the southern mountains; Black Dome east of it; Red Mountain to the southeast looking grand and alone and powerful, though it is not a particularly tall mountain; the low, ridgey humps that are Poison, Buck and Quartz mountains west of Red; and that truly massive massif, wide-shouldered Big Dog Mountain, and more snowy peaks farther south, including Yalakom Mountain and the Shulaps Range. Those last translate to "ewe" and "rams," and the old titles tell us where Churn Creek bighorn ewes did and did not migrate to drop and raise their lambs each year, and where the rams pastured. The ranges beyond all of that blur into themselves. And the whole of it shines, white and mighty, even on that dull and cloud-covered May morning.

There is nothing like the long view to get a good and lasting perspective on your own small place in this great, vast, rolling land we are so privileged to inhabit. And an integral and inevitable part of that perspective is the patchy mass of clear-cuts all the way to the edges of those snow-covered ridges and ranges, not far short of what the eye can see.

The largest patch of all, just down the road, was the great swath of beetle-killed timber, felled, yarded and in the process of being loaded and transported, that stretched the rest of the way to Big Meadow. The last time I had been here, a year earlier, most of that timber was standing, and even with my logging camp upbringing and all that coast logging experience behind me, I was shocked at the extent of the cut. In time, new trees would seed and grow, and feeding ungulates would thrive (for a few years) on the young second growth, but that country was irrevocably changed, and many signs of old human life, old human history, were obliterated for all time.

I detoured down a short branch road, past a lineup of logging machinery and piles of windrowed scrub timber—skinny lodgepole pine mainly—to get a peek down into Big and Little Basins at the big bend up Churn Creek. I could see a series of grassy, hazy, sun-facing slopes down the narrow valley to Wycott Flats. Out on the mainline again, I soon spied pickups through the tree fringe, parked near the Big Meadow cow camp, and turned in for that promised morning coffee and a little more good company. This higher country was still grey and leafless.

Blue smoke was rising from a hunting shack. The first person I noticed was an older man, not heavy, medium tall, with a strong jaw, glasses and long hair in a ponytail under his ball cap. He could only be Percy Rosette. Who else, with that fierce, hawklike visage? The man wore personal authority like a good old shirt. His opening words, uttered with a serious face, were something like "Game warden, not another game warden!"

I was out of the car and introducing myself, shaking his hand, when Larry emerged from the cabin. He quickly assured me that Percy was just having a joke and invited me in for breakfast.

On the way, Larry stopped to show me the new deerhide drum he had made. He explained that it needed to be wakened before it was ready to use and that he hadn't made the beater yet. The octagonal drum head was very tight, the hide stiff and strongly bound, and there were still short deer hairs on the thongs. I rapped the head with my fingers; it made a high, tight, almost singing sound. I noted several tiny stretch marks along the rim. "Nice job, man," I said, with a quick hand on his shoulder. Larry had a right to be proud.

We stepped in. I was introduced to Julia Gilpin, a quiet, smiling, older lady who was Percy's partner. Grandchildren were lined up, helping themselves to hash browns, boiled eggs, fried sausages, rice and good bread: a feast for the multitudes. A tall coffee pot was steaming on the back of the stove. "Grab a cup," Larry said. Mildred was ready for the hungry masses: cups for coffee; a fitted bag full of plastic plates; another container with utensils; a big pot of hot, soapy water for dirty dishes; a receptacle for scraps. Phil, as usual, was busy doing chores, getting things done; he's obviously a good man to have on a trip.

We ate that fine food, drank our coffee, and talked and joked. It seemed everybody there liked to laugh, and laugh we did. I had previously mentioned to Mildred that I was maybe having another book published; the signs so far were looking good. I had a collection of stories all ready about old-timers:

"Did you say it's called Old Lies?"

ranchers and survivors and renegades, land-based people, Native and non-Native, mostly from the Tatlayoko–West Branch area of the southwest Chilcotin. I was still collecting photographs.

"You didn't tell me the name of your new book," she said.

"Old Lives," I replied, giving her the short answer. There was background hubbub.

"What's that?" Percy asked. "Old Lies? Did you say it's called Old Lies?"

I said again, "Old Lives."

"Was that Old Lies?" he repeated, catching on that he had something good going.

Larry, who was already laughing, and I looked at each other. It was one of those moments. I shrugged, and the expression on my face was "Sure, why not? Old Lies is as good a name as any. What the heck, eh." Everybody laughed; Larry was just about killing himself. Over the rest of the morning, he'd mutter "Old Lies" to himself and pick up the laughing all over again. It was infectious.

That Percy Rosette is a fox. He must have said about four times that short morning, in that old-time accent of his, usually as an aside, "You've gotta have humour; you can't get enough humour," as if humour was a basic need to get you through (which, of course, it is). Our respective humours seemed to match. He expressed considerable wonder at this weird and wacky modern, city-dominated and oh-so-fast world we find ourselves in these years. I said that my partner Marne and I, in our approaching old age (well, mine, at least), shake our heads often at the latest foolishness. "Who needs lies?" I called out.

Percy went on to talk about having gone to Weight Watchers. The image of this tough old cowboy and moose hunter in fluorescent spandex in some gym somewhere, doing aerobics in a group, was just too bizarre. The punchline, after drawn-out detail, was that he'd only gone to the café there with a buddy to have a cup of coffee, but now he could say proudly he was "the only Indian in Kamloops to go to Weight Watchers."

We talked of a number of things: the size of that clear-cut ("I thought we weren't allowing massive clear-cutting any more"), more wild places in the backcountry, residential schools, the anthropologist James Teit. Mildred wanted a proper copy of Teit's Secwepemc book; she was frustrated with her photocopied version as some of the printed material was cut off. I said I would see if I could search out a copy for her.

Later, Percy remarked that he thought James Teit got some things wrong. I made no comment at the time, but I recalled that family versions of the old stories, myths and histories, like local histories in general, so frequently differ from each other, family from family, village to village, sometimes substantially, with each version sworn to be the correct one. It's all about who's doing the telling. In his pack-train travels, Teit could only have met and talked with a limited number of informants, and their knowledge would have varied greatly.

On the not-so-simple topic of residential schools, I tend to just listen and nod. There are complexities, differences of opinion, and horrors too tough to get into, and I have little to add to the discussion. Percy was in an explanatory mode, stating, "They were trying to make us obedient, a part of their culture ... Now, we are getting our own culture back." That's what these backcountry trips with the kids were about. I admired his detachment.

We shifted on to talk of old ways, old knowledge and skills, too much of which is lost in our sedentary, near-universal, TV/computer culture. The comprehension of old, hard times and the land-based knowing, application and patience that was fundamental to survival is escaping us. "Time goes by so fast," Mildred said. She stated her regret at not spending more time with her teacher, nodding respectfully, as she did so, to the smiling Julia beside her. Julia is experienced in traditional plant knowledge and uses. Larry asked me if I used old-time medicines at all. I said not especially, but told of a good friend in the lower Similkameen Valley whose slow recovery from severe injuries, multiple operations and chronic pain depended in part on such knowledge. I mentioned her Indian healer, the late Charley Horse Squakin. I could see Mildred wince at the extent of our friend's suffering.

Phil sat down in the open doorway to listen and, perhaps, watch Stobart Creek and the signs outside of early spring. I had the feeling he preferred to be outdoors, that that was the main reason he was out here. I'd heard from Don Logan that Phil's dad, Davey, had died the previous year, and I remarked that his departure must have left a big hole. Phil nodded. I said that my old man had died twelve years earlier and I still missed him; I continue to have questions only he could answer.

"You should show Percy the book," Mildred said. She meant, of course, Don Logan's Canoe Creek book.

Percy had gone outside, and I stepped out to join him. I found him along the edge of the swollen creek close by. We stood side by side, taking in the cool morning and watching the flow of the creek in full flood, a force running dark and smooth and fast out of the high swamps on the south side of Wales Mountain; it would merge with Gaspard Lake a few miles to the northwest. Percy noted how high the creek was and said, "We used to cross it way upstream," gesturing with a wide sweep of his arm.

"So you cowboyed for Gang Ranch then?" I asked.

"Oh yeah," he said, "for a long time."

As a cowboy, he would have been more used to seeing this place later in the season, when the cattle were gathered here at Big Meadow, ready to be pushed out and up to their summer ranges. I concluded that the low, plywood shack we'd just had breakfast in had been used by

So much close familiarity, such concentration.

Rosette family members for years, and they'd camped here long before that. They would have had intimate knowledge of all this backcountry.

We moved over to the cabin, and Percy sat down at a rough table on the warm side to go through the old photos in Don's book. I stood to one

The cabin at Big Meadow. Photo courtesy of Marne St. Claire.

side behind him. He looked at several, taking his time, then half-turned to say happily to me over his shoulder, "I'm gonna be here all day." The sun was shining weakly through clouds, lighting up the willow brush stems and twigs: bright oranges, sharp yellows, reddish browns. The rest of the adults joined us: Mildred sitting next to Percy, close and focused; Julia standing behind with her hand on Percy's back; Larry on the far side. As on the previous evening, they peered, turned pages, conferred, checking each face, each memory, slowly working through the book—so much close familiarity, such concentration. I stood watching and listening. Behind their quiet talk I could hear Stobart Creek in its rush off the slopes, a presence on the other side of the cabin. The kids were playing close by.

Phil joined in the looking and at one point turned to me, almost excitedly, and exclaimed that he'd just spotted a photo of his mother, taken when he was young, that he'd not seen before. His mum, Nora, herself a Rosette, had died prematurely from a quick flu, and I gathered Phil's knowledge of her from his early life was limited.

As I watched and mused, a sense came slowly over me that I might be wrong to keep Don Logan's book for myself. I hesitated a while to listen to my deep gut for knowing, to let a little time test that sense for best truth. Eventually, when I was sure and the moment seemed right, I began to speak. "I've been thinking, Mildred, that you should have the book," I heard myself saying.

She demurred, "No, no ..."

I spoke slowly, my voice low. "Those are not my people; those are your people, Mildred."

I happened to be looking in Larry's direction. As I uttered the words, an expression, like shock, like a physical impulse, almost literally fell down his face and neck, as if flooding in from some deep place. "Then I'll give you my drum," he said, or words close to that, as if he had little say in the matter, as if the choice was reflexive. There was a brief quiet.

"You are too generous, Larry."

"No, no, I'll give you my drum," and he stepped around Percy, Julia and Mildred, his face serious, and shook my hand—first in a hand clasp and then in the Indian way, knuckles first, with the follow-up "like a salmon's tail flapping," like our hands and arms had their own life, like the truth of this moment was absolute, the whole truth of it intrinsic to itself. His hand was big and work-roughened and predictably gentle.

After another pause, Larry said, "The deal is closed when you shake hands." I was feeling the deal to be done. Later, he said again that the drum would need to be wakened, some songs would be sung, and he still needed to make that beater.

Mildred asked if I wanted the photo of Marne and me, part of Don's dedication to us, at the front of the book. "No," I said, half-joking, perhaps a bit thoughtlessly. "When you see it, I want it to remind you of the whole story, including our part in it," or some similarly half-lame, slightly smartass words like that. I was glad I'd completed at least a first read of his book, though I would have liked to study the photos more thoroughly. Don had put so much thought and work into it.

Later, Mildred stopped me and, rather seriously, asked if I could use a fish. As I was saying, "Sure, thank you very much," she handed me a good-sized, still partly frozen trout, neatly wrapped in smooth brown paper, and dated *2010*; I don't remember if she noted the month.

At the back of the cabin, Larry was peeling a willow branch he'd just cut for its new role as a drum beater. I asked him if he'd like a copy of my book about Stranger Wycott and parts of the Chilcotin country. Larry thought that would be "cool." We'd been talking about the upper Big Creek area, and I opened *Stranger Wycott's Place* to a photograph of outfitter Barry Menhinick on old Rabbit, a famous former Gang Ranch horse, with a couple of loaded pack animals. Marne had taken the photo on our 1997 horse trip around the South Chilcotin Mountains; the rounded, glacial defile that held Lorna Lake and Big Creek headwaters made a powerful backdrop for her picture. With hand gestures, I indicated the locations of Tosh and Grant creeks, Iron Pass and especially Graveyard Valley, a place of importance for peoples from both sides of the mountains since before history. The mysterious, and usually untravelled and unseen, Powell Pass might have been mentioned in there somewhere also, or was I just thinking about it wistfully? Larry was familiar with that country, and especially with Graveyard Valley, a place redolent with old stories drifting, almost visible, like smoke on a light wind.

One story, only one of several, some conflicting, says that about the time of the 1918–19 flu epidemics, some people from Stone Reserve in the East Chilcotin were down south hunting. Around Hungry Valley they ran short of food, and by the time they came to what is now Lost Valley, they'd lost track of where they were. Perhaps the weather was bad; certainly the country was wild, with brushy drainages and timbered ridges running in different directions.

The six low mounds in a tight row up Graveyard Valley were becoming hard to discern unless you knew just where to look.

They carried on to what is now named Graveyard Valley, where six members of the party died and were buried. Some sources suggest it was the Spanish flu that carried them off. Their souls were restless, so the old tale goes, and moved on up and over a treeless divide farther to the southeast, to Little Paradise Valley, a beautiful place, rocky, windswept and snowy in the high parts. Big Paradise, in among tall Relay, Cardtable and Castle peaks, is the next valley beyond.

The six low mounds in a tight row up Graveyard Valley were becoming hard to discern unless you knew just where to look. Nearly two decades earlier, when Don and I first walked into the valley to see them, log ends and wood bits still marked the sites. Old photos, taken, I believe, by Big Creek rancher Duane Witte, and only about half a century old, show the graves enclosed by low log fences. Two crosses stood tall above them. Now a single, rough circle of stones delineates the place. Such a location up near tree line, wild and lonely, and a hair spooky, is likely "a place where we pray." There is a long-used campsite, a fire ring, old tether posts on the edge of trees not far away.

I think I heard Larry say that his great-great-grandmother had died and was buried up Little Paradise Creek a long time ago. Later Phil Anderson, his cousin, made a similar statement. Neither Larry nor Phil was sure exactly where the grave was.

In 2008, Don Brooks and I marched from the roadhead out of upper Relay Creek up the Little Paradise horse trail on a too-brief, full day's walk into the alpine. We lost the route for a few minutes in the braided creek beds of the open basin at the top of the valley, but we got a taste. In '09 we walked partway up into the same rocky ridges from the northwest via Little Graveyard Creek, but time cut us short. Little Graveyard joins Big Graveyard not far from the graves site. We have not yet seen Big Paradise Valley, but we have hopes and vague aspirations. Maybe next year.

Larry was stuffing and lashing the leather beater head by this time. Against old stumps, dark trees, last year's grasses and the weatherworn cabin wall, all a uniform shade of grey, the newly skinned beater stick struck me as a thin, pale thing, fresh and naked and starkly vulnerable. With a little smile, Larry made sure I knew that the twine he was using for lashing had prevented his

Slowly, we were gathering for the awakening of the new young drum.

front bumper from falling off his truck; it was a lighthearted joke he was making, but there was a thread of seriousness through it. I was sincerely, if not abjectly, grateful.

Slowly, we were gathering for the awakening of the new young drum. Percy and Larry had been conferring as to right procedures, and Larry had quietly announced earlier that they would sing a hunter's song and a wolf song. The grandkids appeared—I think Phil had something to do with that—and we formed a circle in the warming sun. Julia joined in beside me on my left; Phil was to my right and Mildred was beside him. Larry, with the about-to-be-awakened drum, was across the circle. Percy stood next to him with his own drum, good-sized, well-used, dark. He held it as if its weight was substantial and its authority was of consequence. I noticed Percy had removed his peaked cap and smoked glasses. The grandchildren, Vincent, Challon and Regan, their faces solemn and their bodies still, stood in a row between Larry and Julia. We were all silent. The creek sound was a constant, and the trees were standing, living presences, as always. It was a good day to be drumming, singing and listening.

Then Percy started talking in Secwepemc, Larry translating briefly: the hunting song would be first. They began with a solid beat, not slow, not fast. Then their voices became part of the sound. They knew the song well and it issued forth, steadfast and clear. Our full attention was a part of the song, meditative, surrendering, at once focused and unfocused: what else to do but be in it. I was aware of my head moving, probably imperceptibly, but not intentionally, to the beat. The song came to its end in its own good time—there was no need to hurry—and Percy spoke, through Larry again, announcing that the wolf song would now be sung. The tune was wolves howling; the drumbeats strong hearts beating; the totality, wild Earth. At the song's close, Larry, speaking low, almost in a whisper, said, "Percy, Percy, look, look," indicating the sky in the west behind me. An eagle was circling, an immature baldy, soaring and circling, not far up, curious, called in by the songs maybe, the beat, wanting to know what's what. We observed it watching us for a short while. "The world is always watching," as the Koyukon Dené of North Alaska still say.

Percy and Larry began the last song unannounced, proclaiming the new drum, I'm assuming, though I'm not entirely certain. Before the song commenced, Percy paused and stared ahead for several extended moments, his look short-sighted, piercing. I could swear his eyes in his gaunt face were a pale shade of blue. What did he see? Where did he go?

The wakening song was brief, and, again, the rhythm was strong, the voices true. The power and quality of the deep sound of those beating drums must reverberate through our bodies, our consciousness, the soles of our feet, and link us to the living ground and to all existents, sentient and insentient, within range; we could say that the sound of drums is the sound of land expressing itself. It animates the new drum's heart, announcing its entry into the world of myth time, as true a place as this everyday world we assume to be real.

The last beat died into silence, and I noted a look of sober sadness, just a tinge, about Larry. He leaned in slightly, glanced at me and spoke, his voice tailing off: "Now, you sing the songs back." I think he meant to be joking a little, but there was a tone of resignation, almost sorrow, in his voice, as if singing these songs reached him, as if their antiquity, their gravity, their meaning, had touched and transported him. Where did the songs take him? Into pain? Personal or ancient? Were our respective stories too disparate to truly connect, our people's histories too conflicted to be shared? Had there been some shift in equilibrium in the morning's events that disturbed him?

He handed me the drum; I was honoured. I had already spoken a few brief, hopefully not perfunctory, words of gratitude and acknowledgement, but I felt in his debt and would continue so. Later, Larry reminded me that he and his friends meet here at this place on the same May weekend each year, the suggestion being that I was welcome to join them.

I think of all the events unfolding on that morning when I offered Don Logan's Canoe Creek book to Mildred, and I strive to properly comprehend the sense of obligation that Larry must have experienced in those moments of connection and exchange. There are sensitivities and feelings here that are all but beyond me: sensitivities emerging from our connections with each other, with those places where we were (and still are), with our histories and past practices, and with the sublime delicacy of all life around us. Such sensibilities necessitate respect and acknowledgement on a level of subtlety that is somewhat new to me, and to most, I believe. Good manners involve a constant renewing of balances; Larry, being the intelligent and courteous gentleman that he is, had no choice but to balance the exchanges between us in the best ways he knew.

Sensitivities emerge from our connections with each other, with those places where we were (and still are), with our histories and past practices, and with the sublime delicacy of all life around us.

I wonder, perhaps, if he had doubts that I would take the drum and its implications seriously enough, that I would treat it and all it stood for with appropriate attention. He could well be right about that. I did place the drum in the back of my car rather quickly, and even though it was cool out there in the early spring Gang Ranch outback, I discovered later that the drum head got even tighter and took on new stretch marks. It had become warmer back there than I would have predicted. From then on, when I travelled, I was careful to bury the drum in as cold a place as I could find. Larry's last words to me were "Let me know if the drum head splits; I can make a new one." It did occur to me that the damp coastal cool might suit the drum more.

I am curious whether those songs we were a part of in the sun on that morning, the one referring to hunting, the other to wolves, would have been sung if I had not told Larry that I had been checking for fresh wolf sign in that valley past Augustine's Meadow.

There are mysteries here, little and great, that I only partially understand, but I do know this: *Neech-help* is a connecting place, and that place by Stobart Creek at Big Meadow, probably an old camping site from ancient times, is likely a connecting place as well. And we all—Phil, Mildred, Larry, Julia, Percy, the young grandchildren, the songs, the drums, those places and me—connected naturally and easily. The collective flow of it, subtle and not subtle, was, and is, unimaginably greater than we simple folks alone. Long usage and frequent acknowledgement must help such connections occur. Percy Rosette had said, "There are some places ... where we pray." Well, we pray to know and be a part of these places, to acknowledge and to add to the liveliness. We pray to give thanks and to surrender. When we truly pray (and surrender), we set our souls free, in time.

> *There are mysteries here, little and great, but I do know this: Neech-help is a connecting place.*

I pulled away from the Stobart Creek place with waves of goodbye, turned onto the main road and headed south, hoping to make it the whole way to Beaver Valley. But on a high, dark, north-facing slope with its spruce and lodgepoles still standing, not far short of the Dash Creek crossing and several miles before my destination, I came upon the first real snow, too deep and slippery for the Pathfinder and my all-terrain steel radials to handle. Not especially surprised, I turned around, and turned again at a branch road pointed across upper Churn Creek in the direction of Red Mountain. On my way up, I'd noticed that the usually shut gate was open, and I decided to see where that road would take me.

It had rained a week earlier, and most muddy road margins had hardened since; the road was plugged with animal tracks, most distinct, few mysteries anywhere. I stopped every so often to see what was moving: an occasional black bear out on a first, post-hibernation walkabout; few deer, but several moose crossing the road on their way to swamps and patches of second growth somewhere else; and, mainly, copious sign of wolves, a pack, clearly using the road for a throughway so they could cruise for moose. One animal, I'm sure the alpha male, had huge footprints, only slightly smaller than my wide open hand. At times, the distributions of their tracks suggested the pack was having a good frolic, perhaps a celebration of light and warmth, or of the most recent moose carcass. I could spot no grizzly tracks.

All the while, lone Red Mountain loomed in front of me. I had been up there before from the Yalakom side to the south: on my own the first time; partway up with Bob Whittet; partway up with Marne, a lovely walk; and once, one perfect August day, all the way up with Don Brooks and the help of a nice little staircase near the top. We spent an hour up there, looking covertly down on eleven ewes and lambs, California bighorns, who had migrated up the gulches from lower Churn Creek, no doubt, and were feeding, moving about and cavorting on a large, sloped bench below us. A big, dozing, cud-chewing doe, lower down on a deer-bed facing west, was watching their backs. If those animals knew we were up there, they didn't care.

I drove on until I came to an old moose camp, where a well-worn-in track crossed the road, aimed south at Swartz and Mud lakes, and coming from Windy Ridge, Lone Cabin Creek and Empire Valley in the north. It was barely wide enough now for a horse, but it was old and historic. This was the route opened up half a century ago by cowboys from Empire Valley Ranch, so they could access much-needed summer ranges down around Red Mountain and Poison Mountain meadows, and Relay Creek, and over at Spruce Lake and upper Gun Creek to the southwest. This was the same skinny road Barry Menhinick and son Warren used to drive their horse herds through in the years when they wintered them above Empire Valley on Clyde Mountain. It took them two days from Gold Bridge. Amazing!

But the day was long, I had miles to go, and I was starting to feel weary. I was a long way out there alone, a good two days' hard walk, minimum, should my aging Pathfinder happen to falter or wind up in a ditch. The dark places on the road were still slick; runoff was happening, the swamps were high and there was no traffic at all, not that I expected any. I turned around again and started slowly homeward, studying footprints as I went and looking hard over my shoulder at Red Mountain.

Near Big Meadow on a large, clear-cut flat, nothing but road and short stumps, I spotted a well-used pickup faced in my direction, but the something-wrong-with-the-picture was that he was moving in reverse, slowly, away from me, back down the road. A little breeze had come up, and I quickly realized that the driver, Percy Rosette as it turned out, was chasing down a white plastic bag caught by a wind gust, probably blown out of his own truck box.

The scene reminded me of the old Chinese story of two monks walking up beside a rushing creek to visit a well-known recluse living farther up the mountain. The older of the two was extolling the wisdom of the old man. As he spoke, a bright lettuce leaf came floating down the creek. "He can't be that wise," commented the younger monk. But right behind, tottering creakily down the hillside, who should appear but the old sage himself, staff in hand, obviously bent on catching that lettuce leaf.

We stopped for a brief talk, side windows open, car to car.

"Did you find what you were after?" asked Percy.

"Not really," I said and proceeded to give a short report of my per-egrinations over the previous hours, remembering to include the size of those big wolf paws. "I saw lots of tracks," I said, which causd Julia to throw her head back and laugh as they drove off. I suppose, to her, that translates as "no meat, just tracks."

Days later, after an extended trip out to Tatlayoko–West Branch, and stops at Fletcher Lake, Riske Creek, Williams Lake, Clinton and the Yalakom Valley, I was on the Duffy Lake highway, driving the Pathfinder home. At Clinton, when I told Don and Karen Logan that I had given away my personally dedicated copy of his Canoe Creek book, Don, a generous man, was taken aback, but I suspect he would have done the same as me. Larry Emile's drum was lurking coolly under my sleeping bag in the back of the car.

At the edge of my seeing (that part of our vision where we really see), I was sighting half-hidden rock faces on the mountains above the Joffre Lakes.

I had about reached the divide at the top end of the long Cayoosh Creek drainage. Spring was still slow in these high parts: there was packed snow at road level in the slide chutes, mists covered most of the mountains, a bank of coast rain clouds glowered darkly in the southwest. At the edge of my seeing (that part of our vision where we really see), I was sighting half-hidden rock faces on the mountains above the Joffre Lakes, peaking out through cloud holes, an eye here, a long stony nose there, trying to get a sense of the guy with the new drum most likely. Their countenances were positively animate, unless you stared at them straight on. I guess that's why they call them rock faces.

Two ways, two ways to see.

THIS LAND WE PASS THROUGH

*A myth begins with the assumption that all
existents are alive:
They have identities and appetites and wills,
which necessarily reveal themselves in stories
rather than equations.*

"The Meaning of Mythology"
—Robert Bringhurst

THIS LAND WE pass through has been aboriginal land since myth time, once upon a time. But now we settlers from over several seas, east and west, have arrived here in great numbers with our industrial technology and a driving need for opportunity and space to live. We are here and it looks like we are here to stay. From time's beginning, the human story is much about migration and movement.

The land I pass through on my way to Cariboo–Chilcotin (Tsilhqot'in) country in the south-central interior of British Columbia is Nlaka'pamux (*ink la cap ma*), St'at'imc (*stat lee um*) and Secwepemc (*shuh queck um*)—otherwise known as Thompson, Lillooet and Shuswap—territory. For thousands of post-glacial years, these cultures lived and thrived, and they survive, grow and increasingly thrive here still. Many of the old pre-contact place names remain, and some elders continue to speak and teach the old languages, members of the Salishan family of languages that stretches across the territories from Montana to northwest Oregon and the Bella Coola Valley on the BC mid-coast. The word "Salishan" (Sse'lictcen) is the name the Flathead (Sel'ic) group of speakers, a buffalo-hunting people in western Montana, called themselves.

This is a land of mountains—the Cascade and Coast ranges, the South Chilcotin Mountains, the Marble Mountains west of Clinton, the Cariboo Mountains to the northeast—and big rivers—the great Fraser and Thompson rivers and their tributaries: the Stein, Nicola, Bonaparte, Bridge, Quesnel and Chilcotin. The latter and its various branches drain nearly all the vast Chilcotin Plateau. Mountains and rivers are the background, life blood and essence of our existence up here, and we are of them. At lower elevations, much of the land is covered in grasses: open bunchgrass and big sage benches closer to the Fraser, and grassy meadows studded with dry-belt fir, pine and poplar, cattail and willow farther west. As the rolling plateau gains elevation to the northwest, the country becomes increasingly wooded, and swamp and open wet meadow edges are common. Grassy south-facing slopes and eskers occur throughout. Birds and animals concentrate, and people tended to settle on grassland edges. Life flourishes in the interfaces.

This is a land of mountains and big rivers.

I love this grassland/parkland country. My connection is no doubt due to having lived my most formative and impressionable young years in a somewhat similar, though far less expansive and varied territory up the Thompson River north of Kamloops, where I spent much of my time walking. I walked to and from school down in the valley, and back and forth to our only neighbours, the Schilling family, a quarter mile away, for quarts of milk and for company. Once in a while I went walking just to see what was out there; there was never a doubt that I would find my way home again. For much of that walking time, I travelled those country roads and trails alone.

In the late sixties, when I began coming up to this open Interior country again, the land, especially the wild Chilcotin land west of the Fraser, caught me once more and amplified my being. I became enchanted with its various aspects: the meadowlands; the mountain peaks and slopes; pine, fir and high spruce forests; groves of aspen, golden in the fall; bird-ponds and sloughs; and cottonwood bottoms along the rivers and creeks. I tracked portions of some of the river valleys: the Chilcotin, Taseko, Chilko and Tchaikazan, the Homathko and West Branch (Mosley Creek), Big Creek and Nemaiah, the Klinaklini and Dean, the Atnarko down at the head of the Bella Coola Valley, all in the heart or out there on the edges of the Chilcotin Plateau. Most parts, especially out in the wilder west, were never graced much by permanent settlement, and the signs of older human passage and habitation I came across seemed little more than a natural part of the landscape.

Beyond all the tributary rivers and valleys, it was the Fraser River trough itself, with its dry alluvial benches; its own weather systems; its summer heat; its near-exotic range of bird, animal and plant life; the hints of desert country extending far south; and the great river flowing inexorably at the bottom of the trough that sank its subtle, and not so subtle, hooks into me and elevated my mind and soul. It is the dry air and trembling poplar leaves, the signs of old trails, tracks, campsites and dwelling places, the creatures and curiosities, mysteries and wildness without end that have kept me coming. Now, in my elder years, I continue to travel up here, but with an increased urgency, if not frequency, to more thoroughly know, acknowledge and surrender to the forces of this great land that shapes us.

I sense at the level of myth that this land and the aboriginal people that lived here before and live here now were in a measure of active synchrony with each other. Some First Nations folks may well have maintained the old, land-familiar connections from the past; others may have had to work to regain a connection to that old, timeless, mythologizing way of experiencing the world that we immigrants, spawn of the Enlightenment, had learned to deny and ignore.

However, some immigrant newcomers and many of their children and grandchildren, born, nurtured and attached here, have learned or are learning now that we too are, inevitably, of these western places where we live. Our thoughts, imaginings, travels and work are becoming part of the ongoing maintenance, re-creation and unfolding evolution of this land. None of us, aboriginal or settler, can possibly claim to own it truly, no matter how hard we might pretend otherwise: Can we own our mother? Do we subdivide and fence our bodies? Are our souls for sale? We are coming to know now that we are inseparable from this ground under our feet, and always were; it is a function of having been born here. We are that ground and it is us. We increasingly comprehend the need to acknowledge these places where we are, address and name them, take time with them and allow them to fix themselves more solidly into our collective being. To the extent that we know and practise attending, we learn to hear the old aboriginal stories and allow the evolution of our own stories to tell, including, as time unfolds, myth stories parallel to the ancient tales from before. They emanate through us, ground up, from these myriad western places where we stand, walk and live, lie down and die.

James Teit: Rancher, guide-outfitter, ethnographer and translator. Photo courtesy of the Royal BC Museum.

Of course, this land we pass through is layered deep with stories: place stories, personal and local history stories, and the pre-contact tales and myths from long ago that were passed down by scores of aboriginal elders, or preserved on paper a hundred years ago by such undervalued heroes as the ethnographers James Teit of Spence's Bridge and Franz Boas from Germany via Columbia University in America. They tell us in detail of the old ways and times before the Europeans and Asians and their devastating diseases and new practices were visited upon this continent.

In Distant Time—that is to say, myth time—so the old Nlaka'pamux, St'at'imc and Secwepemc stories say, various culture heroes, transformers or changers from the south, moved through the mountains and up the valleys into the dry interior country. In those primeval times before the coming of the changers, humans and animals were believed to be much the same as each other. Early humans seem to have been foolish and ignorant but could communicate at a basic level with animals; most of what little the people knew, apparently, had been shown them by animals. Human existence was spent in uncertainty and fear, especially of the terrible monsters alive in those days. And some of those primitive proto-humans were cannibals, so the old tales tell us.

The transformers arrived and took it upon themselves to improve, fundamentally and often wondrously, the lives of the human inhabitants living here and there along the valleys and watercourses. They taught humans to hunt animals for food, to make fire and to make clothing for themselves. Some mountains and valleys were reshaped to their present form by these travelling changers to bring about greater balance and refinement of life for the people. Such old mythic personages were essential to the basic function of the first aboriginal cultures, and a reminder now of their existence and nature helps give us context for, and perspective on, life in this land in those old times.

In long-ago myth time, an all-powerful personage, Old-One (Old Man), commissioned Old Coyote, trickster, to travel the country and bring about some of those basic changes. Like others of that particularly tricky class of old-time reality-shifters and changers—Mink, up from Harrison Lake in lower Lillooet country; Raven down on the coast; and all the rest of the pantheon of tricksters in their varying ways across the whole wide world—Old Coyote was mischievous and deceitful and difficult to trust. Such beings were near-totally selfish and on a ceaseless search to gratify their own basic wants and whims; the improvements they brought about were largely incidental and rarely benignly inspired. Old Coyote considered

Coyote. Photo © Chris Harris of Country Life Publishing, author of *Spirit in the Grass.*

himself superior to all around him and frequently tried to do creative, imitative acts that were far beyond his powers. Consequently, he often failed, much of his work was left unfinished and Old-One had to come along later to complete his projects. But Old Coyote was a major force and was responsible for the introduction of many great things including salmon, good fish-catching places on the river banks, the seasons, and day and night. He has disappeared now, somewhere far to the east they say, but he may return some day.

But transformers of goodwill walked this land as well: Old-One, of course, who appeared and moved about in the form of an aged man, and Kokwe'la and the three Qoa'qlqal brothers, who travelled up through here from the lower Fraser River in Distant Time. These beings were almost entirely benevolent and did not behave foolishly like Coyote, and if they appeared to do so, it was for a higher purpose. They either killed the monsters that savaged the peoples or transformed those lethal beings into animals or humans more agreeable and of greater use and value to those early aboriginal peoples.

There were other somewhat lesser changers in this dry Interior country also, including Tlee'sa and his brothers, who hailed from the Kamloops area in southern Secwepemc land. Their mother, who was actually their aunt, seems to have been a wise and compassionate person. She felt badly for the plight of people and told Tlee'sa and his brothers the names of the cannibals that frequented the land and the specific locations where they lived. She instructed Tlee'sa in strategies to kill those evil beings, and this he and his brothers did as they moved through the country, much to the people's relief.

On another venture, the brothers travelled west performing a variety of amazing feats, including one where Tlee'sa took the time to change a poisonous tobacco tree near Deadman Creek into a plant the people could gather and smoke without harm. The brothers continued north along the Bonaparte River, up past where Clinton is now, to the area around Chasm, having encountered and transformed a number of supernatural animals—arrow-stone-owning grizzly bear sisters, a massive elk, a deadly bighorn ram—into creatures less formidable and easier to exploit or hunt and kill for food. West of Hat Creek, past Marble Canyon on the far side of Pavilion Creek, Tlee'sa came upon Tsakelsxene'lxa, a man-killing woman with teeth in her vagina, who was guarded by a dangerous, long-legged, bluish bird named Sokwa'z. Our hero changed Tsakelsxene'lxa into an "ordinary," much more sexually accessible woman with whom he and his brothers would each "have connection." And Sokwa'z became the blue heron we know today.

What is fascinating about Tlee'sa's epic exploits is that, despite his brothers' chronic fears and doubts, he allowed himself at times to be swallowed whole or buried under earth or rocks by some fearsomely large or miraculous creatures—the huge elk, a magic beaver, a lethal marmot— or buried figuratively by a powerful woman as in the Tsakelsxene'lxa encounter. All these predicaments are the equivalent of shamans' journeys down underground tunnels, fraught with toothed dangers in the usual manner, to the underworld where great powers reside. With some assistance from his brothers, Tlee'sa was at all times able to return from these contests with the power of his adversaries much reduced, with his own power increased, and with new practices and resources for the people's benefit, similar to shamans of old. It is as if Tlee'sa and his ilk were enacting the advent of the emerging shamanic age.

Ca'wa, aka Sa'memp, was another transformer-like individual, very wise and good, and capable of magical powers. He was from Churn Creek, not far south of Dog Creek, on the west side of the Fraser River. Ca'wa felt sorry for the plight of some distant peoples beyond Secwepemc home territory and walked throughout their country to show them ways to better their lives. He taught some of the folks he came across to recognize and catch lake fish and make the necessary tools to do so effectively. Ca'wa also demonstrated to some other people, likely Cree far to the northeast, how to sleep properly and how to manage childbirths in an appropriate and healthy manner; their old methods were grossly misguided and unsafe. In a land of Coyote-people who used tree-branch knotholes for sex, a system clearly less than effective for the production of much-hoped-for offspring, he showed them the greatly superior method of intercourse with women. Following this feat, Ca'wa declared firmly that "never again would men need branches for wives," and he returned home to Churn Creek, where he was mightily respected and where he lived to a deserved grand old age.

Ca'wa must surely have lived near the site where, in more recent and prosaically historic times, William "Stranger" Wycott pre-empted and settled a few miles up Churn Creek. The process of mythologizing may well be occurring around that region now as old stories about a variety of Cariboo–Chilcotin legendary figures, pre- and post-contact, including Wycott and his family, slowly transform into myth. Could it be that some of Wycott's aboriginal relatives by his marriage to Maggie Kwonsenak, a Secwepemc woman from Canoe Creek, told him the old Ca'wa tales a century or more ago?

Such tales typically involved Old Coyote's incessant randiness, somebody else's good-looking young wife, and the predictable fracas that followed.

Several of the many Coyote stories that abound are not only about Old Coyote himself, but about his son Three-Stones (Kalla'llst) as well. Such tales typically involved the ever-wily Old Coyote's incessant randiness, somebody else's good-looking young wife or wives, and the predictable fracas that followed. The Kalla'llst reference is noteworthy in that Phil Grinder, an early settler in the Big Bar Creek–Jesmond area, was married to Nancy Kala'llst at about the same time that Joe Kala'llst (or Kalalest), undoubtedly her relative, was chief (presumably the last) of the Secwepemc people living west of the Fraser. His son Alex came to own and run a small ranch up Gaspard Creek, right next to where Gaspard Camp is now. Like most other small ranchers, Alex needed to work away for wages from time to time, frequently for Frank Armes of Dog Creek Ranch, where he was well known and liked for his good character and ready laugh. The Gang Ranch finally bought Alex's outfit in the mid-fifties after years of efforts to squeeze him out. The long-abandoned log buildings still stand, black against the pale grassland behind them, and there is a little, fenced, family graveyard just down the valley. But memories of Alex Kalalest live on in a wooded mountain called Mount Alex not far south of the old place, in a small lake named Alex nearby, as well as in the remains of an aging hunting cabin in the Whitewater country west of Big Creek, which old-timers referred to as Alex's cabin. Is it too strange to ask if these various good people carrying the Kalla'llst name in historic times can be traced all the way back to trickster Old Coyote himself?

This land we are passing through now, where transformers and tricksters walked, was a world of spirits underlying: guardian spirits, giants, dwarfs, and land and water mysteries of all kinds, subtle and powerful. The animals had spirit-worlds of their own to go to underground, with concealed entrances like shaman's tunnels. Some of those entrances were known to certain human individuals. And there was a twilight land somewhere out on the edges of existence where souls went. Ghosts are the shadows of souls.

Mainly, those changers in the old timeless here-and-now myth days were avatars, angel-like characters whose natures were reflective of these western places where they walked. Old Man seems to have been the most powerful and roamed and transformed far and wide. He was a vital force as far east as Kootenay (Ktunaxa) country and Blackfoot (Siksikau), Blood (Kainaiwa) and Piegan (Pikuni) land in what is now southern Alberta and northwest Montana, where he was known as Na'pi, and where he seems to have taken on some trickster qualities. Here transformer Old Man created the usual wide array of benefits and changes for early plains peoples: landscape details, grass, roots and berries, animals and birds, tools and weapons, and even the phenomena of death.

On the lee side of the shining Rocky Mountains in Alberta, the Oldman River runs east to join the Bow River; that name is likely indicative of Old Man's passage through that land. In southwest Saskatchewan, an expanse of grassy ridge called Oldman on his Back has been recently protected; no doubt that country was similarly crossed by transformer Old Man. And there is an Oldman Creek, a tributary of the Athabasca River, north of Jasper.

Nearer to home, in the shadow of the Cascade Range southwest of Princeton in southern British Columbia, on the old aboriginal routes we now refer to as the Hope and Dewdney trails, there are three low mountains in a row, near Hope Pass, known as the Three Brothers. I wonder if this land had been visited by the wandering transformer brothers Qoa'qlqal. Why not? These mountains stand adjacent to Nlaka'pamux territory, where the Qoa'qlqals performed many wonderful acts beneficial to the people up and down the Fraser River.

When we cross the Fraser River and pass through the lands of the Tsilhqot'in to the west, we can encounter transformer/trickster stories from myth time unfolding out there, if our ears and hearts are open. Some of the best-known of these stories come down to us through Livingston Farrand of the Jesup North Pacific Expedition from about 1900 and feature the adventures of Tsilhqot'in cultural hero and transformer Lendix'tcux and his three sons. Such tales parallel myth stories common to the Tsilhqot'in's Secwepemc neighbours and predecessors to the east, suggesting common roots. The exploits of Lendix'tcux are similar to those of Tlee'sa, right down to being swallowed by a giant moose and a deadly beaver, overcoming various human-killing animals, turning himself into a dog (as Tlee'sa saw necessary at one point) and travelling about the eastern half of Chilcotin country doing good deeds and taking the usual risks. On one long and complicated adventure, Lendix'tcux heads off with his sons up the Chilko River to that great mountain lake of the same name. His protracted struggles with the giant beaver there take them all over the backcountry from Chilko Lake down to Siwash Bridge near where their trip began, then up to the icy blue headwaters of the Taseko (Whitewater) Lakes and back down again. In other words, they covered some tough territory. Nowadays Lendix'tcux and his sons can be seen as four stone pillars down the lower Chilcotin River, much like Tlee'sa and his brothers, who were turned to stone by the dancing, pubescent Chipmunk girl (who their mother had forgotten to warn them about) at a place called Slemmi'x, below High Bar, on the mid-Fraser.

Farther west beyond the snowy heights of the Coast Range, Raven stories paralleling those of Old Coyote moved up out of the Bella Coola Valley on the West Coast into the Interior. This extension of Raven's influence is no surprise given that the Nuxalk ancestors of prominent families at Ulkatcho Lake—the Squinas, West, Capoose, Cahoose and Stillas families mostly—emigrated up the grease trails onto the Chilcotin Plateau in early contact times, bringing their stories and practices with them. Nusq'lst, at the mouth of Noosgulch Creek, a few miles west of the foot of the Ulkatcho summer trail, near the present bridge crossing, is the original home village of the majority of those early, east-bound emigrants. In more modern times, their descendents moved south to Anahim Lake. To the southeast near Towdystan, on a massive, at times elusive, boulder hidden in lodgepole pine woods on the far side of an old snake fence, is a bright red ochre painting of Raven in human form with a big mouth full

Rock painting of Raven on a massive boulder southeast of Towdystan in the West Chilcotin. Photo courtesy of Marne St. Claire.

of pointed teeth, to remind us that he has become an enduring West Chilcotin presence.

Myth happens. Trans-formations occur. The genius of myth is that its context can only be greater than us; it is at essence wild and mercifully beyond our con-trol. We cannot choose to tell or write a new myth no matter how determined our intentions. Rather, it is myth that tells (or writes) us, and likely always will. And yet the process of mythologizing emerges from our collective consciousness and actions, our journeys and the stories that we tell, if told regularly and honestly enough. Our lives can take on elements of the mythic over time, in spite of ourselves. Myth stories tell us who we are, where we have been, what we have done and what is possible, if we pay steady attention.

These are difficult times that sorely try our souls. The issues of the future of life in all its diverse forms upon this Earth, and threats to our ultimate survival here, complex beyond our comprehension, seem past our capacities to solve right now. Especially as we are so distracted by our needs to buy, consume and control, and by the demands of day-to-day maintenance. But if we stop long enough to listen carefully to ourselves and to each other, deep down, heart to heart, with our intellects engaged, we must surely know that sweet reason or our ideology of choice alone will not do it; good intentions and hard work alone are not enough. It's a wild world out there, and our usual rote, impulse and survival-driven practices, so typically short-term, so commonly retarded by ego, individual and collective, give us scant chance to manage it all.

The world of myth is a both/and world. That is its basic nature. The process of mythologizing incorporates two ways to see and is all the more whole-minded and intelligent for that. Two ways to see, two layers of understanding: the layer we all know—the empirical, rational way; the outer, summer layer of doing and measuring and proving; the way of science, industry and production—and the other layer—the darker, inner, winter layer; the layer of transformation and transcendence; the quantum layer of myth, myth land, myth time and myth stories; the realm of "the long present" where past and future are but facets of the eternal now. Each layer of awareness is a complement to, a perspective on, a context for, a baseline of understanding for the other. Together they are the beginnings of a totality of body-mind intelligence. Can we become sufficiently inclusive in our awareness that we view the world from both perspectives as a matter of course?

There are, as always, more questions. Can we learn to recognize and know mythologizing when it happens? Like all other existents on this Earth, sentient and insentient, myth stories prefer to be acknowledged. Does Earth have something to say to us about it all? And how would we know when Earth or its various constituents speak, and what are they saying? Would we hear them? Feel them? Are we sufficiently humble? Authentic? Open? Can we be kind? Can we commit to do least harm? Or do the old belief systems and closed modes of seeing and being we cling to so stubbornly, so habitually, limit us and continue to impede our possibilities?

Now wait. Look. Look out there on the far side of all this talk and tell me: is that Old-One I see coming slowly up the road, taking his own sweet time? Old-One all bent over? Is it Old-One out walking, wearing his Coyote mask maybe, his original Buddha-nature covered up like a dog's scratchings beside a bush. Or is it Old Coyote-trickster himself, out playing in an Old Man mask he found or stole somewhere? He's a tricky one, that Coyote—*aren't you, Coyote, eh?* Could it be those old-time quantum changers can help us out of this mess we find ourselves in these days? Or their 21st-century equivalents maybe, in any shape-shifting, modern-day way they choose to display themselves, same as in the old myth days? Can they, can we, slay or subdue the ravening, slavering monsters of ignorance, fear, hard-heartedness, greed, cynicism, and separation that beset us now? Is some new balancing happening here? Could new beginnings come to pass? Where can these stories, ancient and current, out of Cariboo–Chilcotin country take us? What might they show us, out here in this wild land we pass through, where life is powerful and frequently beautiful, where even the bedrock is lively, where mountain ranges shift and move, and most mountains know something and have stories to tell, if we mind our manners, show appropriate deference and learn to listen?

Or are we out here all on our own, alone?

This is a prayer I am asking, in all humility, you understand.

Myths are stories that investigate the nature of the world from the standpoints of the world.

"The Meaning of Mythology"
—Robert Bringhurst

206

ACKNOWLEDGMENTS AND PHOTO CREDITS

IN WRITING ABOUT people, places and events in the Chilcotin backcountry, I inevitably rely on the generous assistance and support of a great many folks, many of whom are or have become good friends.

I must especially thank those fine people who sat down with me and talked, answered questions, shared a pot of coffee, and who eventually, one way or another, made their way onto the pages of these stories. In particular, I refer to the Voght family from Coldwater, Georgina, Tim, Jordan and Tim Jr.; the Hances, David, Roger and Mrs. Hance, and Francis Adams and Sarah Ann, on that shiny spring day back in 2001; Katie and Joe Schuk of Tatlayoko Valley; Bev and Lee Butler and the young Butlers, Chris, Kathy and Lea the fiddler, down in West Branch; the Lulua sisters, Doris and Madeline (whom I never actually met); my brother Chris; fellow traveller and wine aficionado Don Brooks, who goes all the way back with me to 1963 and with whom I've been walking since 1976; Mildred Kalelest, Phil Anderson and the generous drum maker Larry Emile from Canoe Creek; Percy Rosette and Julia Gilpin; and over these now many years "Chilcotin Sage" Birchwater, an emerging legend in his own "write."

Likewise, for the myriad ways in which you have added your kind support, I am grateful to all the folks out there in your various backcountry corners: Iris Moore and Dennis Redford of Driftwood Camp at Tatlayoko Lake; Ria and Hennie Van Der Klis of Chilcotin Lodge at Riske Creek; Veera Bonner at Fletcher Lake; the Warren and Casie Menhinick family at Gun Creek; the "Clinton Logans," Don and Karen, a special thank-you to you, Don, for the personalized copy of *Canoe Creek*; and a special thank-you also to Van Andruss and Eleanor Wright from the Yalakom Valley for including several *Old Lives* stories in *Lived Experience*, your annual literary journal. In the wild world of books, I thank Transmontanus editor, friend and fine writer Terry Glavin; Rolf Maurer and Stefania Alexandru of New Star Books; my new publisher Vici Johnstone of Caitlin Press; and crack copy editor Audrey McClellan. And my thanks to you, Rolf, for allowing us to re-use the *Stranger Wycott* Chilcotin map.

A number of friends and associates have helped me gather the excellent photographs that grace the pages of *Old Lives*. Again, I am deeply grateful to Sage, for according me access to his fine photo collection; Veera Bonner, for permitting me a copy of her classic photo-portrait of Chiwid; Joe and Katie Schuk and Bev and Lee Butler, who loaned me family pictures to copy. As well, Chris Harris of Country Light Publishing; Damon West of Damon West Photography; and Chris Genovali and Jane Woodland of Raincoast Conservation Foundation have all kindly allowed me the use of several of their outstanding animal photographs. Brother Chris and my lovely partner Marne provided the greatest number of photos for *Old Lives*; and old friends Tom Hueston and Peter Stein contributed a picture or two also. I am appreciative of all of you for your generosity.

I am equally grateful for my long-time (I won't say "old") Victoria friends, fellow walkers, family members and good souls: Tom, Trevor, Peter, Bob W., Bruce Ruddell, Bob and Mary Steele, David and Samantha, Michael and Jenny, my brothers Chris and Andrew, and above all, my heart companion Marne. Other friends and supporters include Stuart McLaughlin, Dana Devine, Ken and Joy Schilling, Louise Smith, Gerry

John and Marne enjoying a quiet summer sundowner at the corrals by Big Eagle Lake. Photo courtesy of Marne St. Claire.

and Sharon Betts, Debbie and Glen Stevenson and that lover of BC lore, and fine writer, Theresa Kishkan from the Sunshine Coast. Thank you all.

And here's to James Teit, Emily Lulua Ekks, Donald Ekks, Casimil Lulua, Annie Nicholson, Helen and Ed Schuk and all the other old-timers who have passed on through. I acknowledge and honour you for being "Old Lives in the Chilcotin Backcountry."

I must gratefully acknowledge, also, Howard Norman, author of *Crow Ducks and Other Wandering Talk*, and Gary Snyder, mentor, grey eminence and great writer and poet. Especially, I acknowledge the muses and express my gratitude to them for showing up, staying around and informing me when I am on track.

Any mistakes that survived these many exchanges are mine.

RESOURCES AND FURTHER READING

ANTHROPOLOGY/MYTHOLOGY

Bierhorst, John. *The Mythology of North America*. New York: William Morrow, 1985.

Boas, Franz. Introduction. In *Traditions of the Thompson River Indians of British Columbia,* collected by James Teit. Boston: Houghton, Mifflin, 1898. Reprint, New York: Kraus, 1969.

———. *Geographical Names of the Kwakiutl Indians*. Columbia University Contributions to Anthropology, Volume 20. New York: Columbia University Press, 1934. Facsimile of the first edition. New York: AMS Press, 1969.

Bouchard, Randy, and Dorothy Kennedy, eds. *Lillooet Stories*. Sound Heritage, vol. 6, no. 1. Victoria: Provincial Archives of British Columbia, 1977.

Bringhurst, Robert. *A Story as Sharp as a Knife*. Vancouver: Douglas & McIntyre, 1999.

———. "The Meaning of Mythology." In *Everywhere Being Is Dancing*. Kentville, NS: Gaspereau Press, 2007.

Brody, Hugh. *The Other Side of Eden*. Vancouver: Douglas & McIntyre, 2000.

Campbell, Joseph. *The Power of Myth*. New York: Doubleday, 1988.

Corner, John. *Pictographs in the Interior of British Columbia*. Self-published, 1968.

Day, David, ed. *Myth and the Mountains*. Sound Heritage, vol. 4, no. 3. Victoria: Provincial Archives of British Columbia, 1976.

Duff, Wilson. *The Indian History of British Columbia*. Victoria: Provincial Museum of British Columbia, 1964.

Farrand, Livingston. *Traditions of the Chilcotin Indians*. Volume 2, part 1, of *The Jesup North Pacific Expedition*, ed. Franz Boas. 1900. Reprint, New York: AMS Press, 1975.

Glavin, Terry. *Nemiah: The Unconquered Country*. Vancouver: New Star Books, 1992.

Guss, David, ed. *The Language of Birds*. San Francisco: North Point Press, 1985.

Harner, Michael. *The Way of the Shaman*. New York: Harper and Rowe, 1980.

Hymes, Del. "Mythology." In Volume 7 of *Handbook of North American Indians*, ed. Wayne Suttles. Washington, DC: Smithsonian Institution, 1990.

Lutz, John S. "The Tsilhqot'in." In *Makuk*. Vancouver: UBC Press, 2008.

Maud, Ralph. *A Guide to B.C. Indian Myth and Legend*. Vancouver: Talonbooks, 1982.

Neihardt, John G. *Black Elk Speaks*. Lincoln: University of Nebraska Press, 1961.

Nelson, Richard. *Make Prayers to the Raven*. Chicago: University of Chicago Press, 1983.

Snyder, Gary. "The Incredible Survival of Coyote." In *The Old Ways*. San Francisco: City Lights Books, 1977.

Teit, James. *Traditions of the Thompson River Indians of British Columbia*. Boston: Houghton, Mifflin, 1898. Reprint, New York: Kraus, 1969.

———. *The Lillooet Indians.* Volume 2, part 5, of *The Jesup North Pacific Expedition*, ed. Franz Boas. 1906. Reprint, New York: AMS Press, 1975.

———. *The Shuswap.* Volume 2, part 4, of *The Jesup North Pacific Expedition*, ed. Franz Boas. 1909. Reprint, New York: AMS Press, 1975.

———. *The Thompson Indians of British Columbia.* Volume 1, part 4, of *The Jesup North Pacific Expedition*, ed. Franz Boas. 1909. Reprint, New York: AMS Press, 1975.

Tepper, Leslie, ed. *The Bella Coola Valley: Harlan I. Smith's Fieldwork Photographs, 1920–1924.* Ottawa: Canadian Museum of Civilization, 1991.

BRITISH COLUMBIA HISTORY

Harris, Bob. "Turner Lakes and Hunlen Falls." In *The Best of B.C.'s Hiking Trails.* Vancouver: Maclean Hunter, 1986.

Hoagland, Edward. *Notes from the Century Before.* New York: Ballantine Books, 1969.

Leslie, Susan, ed. *In the Western Mountains.* Sound Heritage, vol. 8, no 4. Victoria: Provincial Archives of British Columbia, 1980.

Lillard, Charles, and Terry Glavin. *A Voice Great Within Us.* Transmontanus 7. Vancouver: New Star Books, 1998.

Lindsay, F.W. *The BC Outlaws.* Kelowna, BC: Orchard City Press & Calendar, 1963.

Morice, A.G. *The History of the Northern Interior of British Columbia.* 1904. Reprint, Smithers, BC: Interior Stationery, 1978.

Neering, Rosemary. *Down the Road.* Vancouver: Whitecap Books, 1991.

Reksten, Terry. *The Illustrated History of British Columbia.* Vancouver: Douglas & McIntyre, 2001.

Rothenburger, Mel. *The Wild McLeans*. Victoria: Orca Books, 1993.

Shelford, Arthur and Cyril. *We Pioneered*. Victoria: Orca Books, 1988.

Sherwood, Jay. *Surveying Central British Columbia*. Victoria: Royal BC Museum, 2007.

Smith, Jessie Ann, as told to J. Campbell and A. Ward. *Widow Smith of Spence's Bridge*. Merritt, BC: Sonotek, 1989.

Whittemore, Scott. "Turner Lake Canoe Chain." In *Hikes in Tweedsmuir Park*. Bella Coola, BC: Self-published, 1994.

Williams, Judith. *High Slack*. Transmontanus 5. Vancouver: New Star Books, 1996.

Woolliams, Nina G. *Cattle Ranch: The Story of the Douglas Lake Cattle Company*. Vancouver: Douglas & McIntyre, 1979.

LOCAL (CARIBOO–CHILCOTIN) HISTORY

Birchwater, Sage. *Chiwid*. Transmontanus 2. Vancouver: New Star Books, 1995.

———. "A Century of Life, Give or Take a Year or Two." Obituary for Lucy (Dagg) Dester Sulin. *Williams Lake Tribune*, May 31, 2001.

———. *Valleau*. Unpublished, 2004.

———. "Helen and Katie Schuk." In *Casual Country '07* supplement, *Williams Lake Tribune*, 2007.

———. "Chilcotin Time." In *Free Spirit: Stories of You, Me and BC*, ed. Gerry Truscott. Victoria: Royal BC Museum, 2008.

———. "Bob and June Draney." In *Casual Country '09* supplement, *Williams Lake Tribune*, 2009.

———, ed. *Gumption and Grit*. Halfmoon Bay, BC: Caitlin Press, 2009.

———. "Emily Lulua Ekks" and "Josephine Gregg." In *Gumption and Grit*. Halfmoon Bay, BC: Caitlin Press, 2009.

Collier, Eric. *Three Against the Wilderness*. Toronto: Clarke, Irwin, 1959.

Davis, Clark. "Traditions Regarding Pictographs at Towdystan, B.C." In *Western Canadian Journal of Anthropology* 2, no. 1 (1970): 89–93.

French, Diana. *The Road Runs West*. Madeira Park, BC: Harbour, 1994.

Hamm, Bert. *My Momentous Moments in the Chilcotin and Vanderhoof Area*. Self-published, 1998.

Hobson, Rich. *Grass beyond the Mountains*. Toronto: McClelland and Stewart, 1951.

Jenkins, Will. *Chilcotin Diary*. Surrey, BC: Hancock House, 1997.

Kopas, Cliff, with Leslie Kopas. *No Path But My Own*. Madeira Park, BC: Harbour, 1996.

Logan, Don. *Dog Creek: 100 Years*. Trafford, 2007.

Mack, Clayton, with Harvey Thommasen, ed. *Bella Coola Man*. Madeira Park, BC: Harbour, 1994.

Orchard, Imbert, interviewer. *The Trail to Bella Coola*. People in Landscape Series. Victoria: Provincial Archives of British Columbia, 1969.

Peterson, Christine. *The Lure of the Chilcotin*. Self-published, 2005.

St. Pierre, Paul. *Chilcotin Holiday*. Vancouver: Douglas & McIntyre, 1984.

Stangoe, Irene. *Cariboo-Chilcotin, Pioneer People and Places*. Surrey, BC: Heritage House, 1994.

Tatla Lake School Heritage Project. *Hoofprints in History*, vols. 1–8. Tatla Lake, BC: Tatla Lake Elementary Junior Secondary School, 1986–2000.

Witte Sisters [Veera Bonner]. *Chilcotin: Preserving Pioneer Memories*. Surrey, BC: Heritage House, 1995.

Woodward, John, and Halle Flygare. *In the Steps of Alexander Mackenzie*. Kelowna, BC: Nature Conservancy of Canada, 1981.

NATURAL HISTORY

Campbell, R.W., N.K. Dawe, I. McTaggert-Cowan et al. *The Birds of British Columbia*, Volume 2. Victoria: Royal BC Museum, 1990.

Cannings, Richard and Sydney. *British Columbia: A Natural History*. Vancouver: Greystone Books, 1996.

Harris, Chris. *Spirit in the Grass*. 105 Mile Ranch, BC: Country Life Publishing, 2007.

Hatler, David, David Nagorsen, and Alison Beal. *Carnivores of British Columbia*. Victoria: Royal BC Museum, 2008.

Lyons, C.P., and W. Merilees. *Trees, Shrubs and Flowers to Know in British Columbia and Washington*. Vancouver: Lone Pine, 1995.

McTaggart-Cowan, Ian, and C.J. Guiguet. *Mammals of British Columbia*. Victoria: Provincial Museum of British Columbia, n.d.

Murie, Olaus. *A Field Guide to Animal Tracks*. Boston: Houghton, Mifflin, 1954.

National Geographic Society. *Birds of North America*. Washington, DC: National Geographic, 1983.

Parish, R., R. Coupe, and D. Lloyd. *Plants of Southern Interior, British Columbia*. Vancouver: Lone Pine, 1996.

Russell, Andy. *Grizzly Country*. Vancouver: Douglas & McIntyre, 1967.

Shackleton, David. *Hoofed Mammals of British Columbia*. Vancouver: UBC Press, 1999.

Turner, Nancy J. *Food Plants of British Columbia*. Part 2, *Interior People*. Victoria: Royal BC Museum, 1978.

Van Tighem, Kevin. *Bears*. Vancouver: Altitude, 1996.

Wooding, Frederick H. *Wild Mammals of Canada*. Toronto: McGraw-Hill Ryerson, 1982.

GENERAL LITERATURE

Aitken, Robert. *The Mind of Clover*. San Francisco: North Point Press, 1984.

Bringhurst, Robert. "Breathing through the Feet: An Autobiographical Mediation." In *Pieces of Map, Pieces of Music*. Toronto: McClelland and Stewart, 1986.

Dogen, Eihei. "The Mountains and Rivers Sutra." In *The Mountain Spirit*, ed. Michael Tobias and Harold Drasdo. Woodstock, NY: Overlook Press, 1979.

LaChapelle, Dolores. *Earth Wisdom*. Silverton, CO: Finn Hill Arts, 1978.

Lillard, Charles. *Cultus Coulee*. Surrey, BC: Sono Nis Press, 1971.

McCarthy, Cormac. *No Country for Old Men*. New York: Random House, 2005.

McLuhan, T.C. *Touch the Earth*. Toronto: New Press, 1971.

Ottaway, David B., and Joe Stephens. "Big Green: Inside the Nature Conservancy." *Washington Post*, May 2003.

Snyder, Gary. *Turtle Island*. New York: New Directions Books, 1974.

———. "Blue Mountains Are Constantly Walking." In *The Practice of the Wild*. San Francisco: North Point Press, 1990.

———. "On the Path, Off the Trail." In *The Practice of the Wild*. San Francisco: North Point Press, 1990.

INDEX